That Which I Have Seen, Heard, and Experienced

A Memoir
by John Neufeld

From Russia to Canada...

with commentary and annotations
by Gerald Neufeld

Dedication

*To the memory of Louise and John Neufeld,
Mom and Dad, who sacrificed much
so that we could live a life of fulfillment
in peace and security in Canada.*

Contents

A Foreword with Acknowledgements

During the lockdown periods of the COVID19 Pandemic of 2020 to 2022, Johann (John) Neufeld's memoir gave me, his fourth child, an opportunity to meet my father at a much deeper level than I had experienced him during my childhood and youth. Dad was a man of few words, but there were occasions when he did speak about his childhood in "Russia," present-day Ukraine. However, I heard little about his life in Canada, begun in 1926 at age 21. Having many hours to transcribe Dad's written words electronically onto my computer, first in German and then in English with my sister Linda's translation, I often found myself working through tears as I read his accounts of loss and survival. But through all the tribulations and losses during his childhood, Dad constantly lived a life of gratitude for what he believed was divine guidance and purpose in his life.

Dad was born in 1905 in a prosperous region of the Russian empire, now Ukraine, in what was one of the many colonies of Germanic and European peoples that had settled in that region beginning at the end of the 18th century. He died in October of 1993. The evening before his death, I sat with him for an hour in quiet conversation between periods of silence, just two weeks after the loss of Elizabeth, my life's partner, through separation. As Dad and I briefly spoke about my situation, he simply said, "I think everything will work out for the best." I have come to realize that his trust in the goodness of God's grace and a firm belief that our lives will unfold for the best has often given me strength and courage during difficult times. He taught me to be grateful for a lifetime of many wonderful gifts.

A memoir provides an opportunity for the writer to reveal the memories and innermost thoughts that forged his personal narrative during a lifetime of experiences. Having lived with Dad's memoir for many months during the past two years, and while reading it many times, I felt compelled to add historical background to his memory of events that were part of major changes in the history of the European world during the early 20th century. I also decided to add some memories of conversations with Dad and Mom that were pertinent to the events about which Dad wrote in his memoir. My memories of those conversations must be seen through the lens of my perspective on events and conversations from the past. (Perhaps it goes without saying that all history is written from the perspective of the writer or the one who compiles the writings of others.)

In transcribing Dad's German writing of his memoir into electronic print, I took the liberty of adding contemporary German words (with explanations) for some German words in use by the Mennonite community in Russia. Dad's German sometimes reads like a nineteenth-century use of the language that was much influenced by a Mennonite dialect and, perhaps, his reading of the German in Gothic print in a large wellworn Bible that he kept close to him all his life. (A PDF copy of Dad's memoir in German can be had by contacting me at gneufeld@uwo.ca.) Linda translated Dad's memoir many years ago keeping the nuance and manner of the Mennonite German way of speaking. I am very grateful for her work on the English translation that forms the basis for Dad's memoir in this book.

Edgar Rogalski, Dad's sister Anna (Neufeld) Rogalski's son, translated Grandma Barbara Neufeld's diary. I have interwoven many sections of that diary with John Neufeld's memoir. Her diary was written during the time of immigration and during the family's early years in the Beaverlodge area of northern Alberta. Edgar also generously contributed to the various genealogical aspects of the material in this book. Mary (Thiessen) Smith and Bernie Thiessen (daughter and son of Dad's sister Maria) supplied materials that are included in this book. Conversations with them have added depth to my understanding of the family narrative in this book. The contributions of these special cousins added much to Dad's memoir.

Hugo Peters (Linda's husband) has written a very concise overview of Mennonite history that I have taken the liberty to quote. Thank you, Hugo, for instilling a renewed interest in me to learn more about Anabaptist history and the rather remarkable people that came from many parts of Europe contributing their theological ideals and ethical principles that shaped who our parents were and the beliefs by which they lived.

Last, but certainly not least, I am grateful for the many conversations with Linda, Arnold, and Dan regarding our parents. Some of my comments, interspersed between Dad's writings, reflect those conversations.

Finally, I give a special thanks to Pat who lovingly encouraged me to record the Neufeld story for future generations. She also had parents who left war-torn countries, those of Hungary and England, after World War II to begin a new life in Canada. Each of us, whoever our parents may be, brings a story of perseverance, hard work, and love of family and country to our shared Canadian heritage.

The impetus for putting Dad's memoir in a book was a desire to have our children know more about their ancestry. To that end, Jerome and Nicole and their spouses, Sharon and Mike, were often in my mind as I read about life in Russia (now Ukraine) over a hundred years ago. (Mike Hryn's paternal grandparents also emigrated from the Ukraine.) Our grandchildren, Cayley, Miles, Wendell, Holden, and Clint are also the reason for this effort. It is they who may some day wonder from where their ancestors came, what kind of people they were, and what shaped their world view and how they lived. Some day their children may also read John Neufeld's account of life in Russia, his family's immigration and beginnings in a new land, their countless relatives, and marvel at how the world they live in has changed from that of their great grandparents and great, great grandparents.

What induced the Neufeld and the Enns families to leave "Russia" and emigrate to Canada when many of their neighbours refused to leave their paradise of many generations? Was it to seek economic advantage in a new world? No. It was because they loved freedom—the freedom to worship God in the manner that they felt was appropriate. It was the freedom NOT to bear arms in a conflict. It was freedom from fear and the oppression that they experienced after the Russian revolution and what they might experience with the encroachment of collectivization and Communist suppression of their way of life, their language, and their religion. We all owe them much gratitude for their decision to emigrate to Canada those many years ago.

Gerald Neufeld, November 2022

Introduction

John Neufeld's story is just one account of the many people who found refuge in this wonderful country we call Canada. Canada, in a nutshell (or a maple leaf?), is a gathering of people from all lands of the earth with names that come together like tributaries flowing into rivers of partnership that often run deeper than bloodlines. It is a story of people who weathered difficult circumstances to arrive at the happy realization that they too could become citizens of Canada. We, the children of immigrants, have the good fortune to have been born in Canada where old prejudices and practices are replaced with patterns of friendship and co-operation with each new generation.

We won the birth lottery. Yes, we did. During the COVID-19 pandemic years of 2020 and 2021 you would have heard that comment often during Pat and my daily five-kilometre walks through the University of Guelph Arboretum and Turfgrass Institute lands. There we enjoyed the air, the sky, the trees, and the flowers during a time of uncertainty. How did Pat Eton-Neufeld, born Patricia Esztelecky, become the loving and much-loved grandmother to Cayley, Miles, and Wendell Neufeld and Holden and Clint Hryn? "Grandma Pat" (whose mother was from Liverpool and whose father was from Szeged in Hungary) married me when she was 40, her first marriage. But that story, woven into the fabric of the Neufeld story, is for later. This is a story of how the Neufeld family left a farm in the pleasant village of Marienthal in southern Russia to create a whole new life in Canada.

My parents grew up in a time, place and culture that is as foreign to me as Asia is to North America. My father, born June 6, 1905, had already celebrated his 44th birthday when I was born on September 20, 1949, in Tofield, Alberta. At his age, Dad, already somewhat worn with decades of hard labour and years in his position as the leading minister in the Tofield Mennonite Church, was often more like a grandfather to me than the father I longed to have. Some of my classmates, whose fathers were not much more than 20 years old when they were born, had grandfathers that were my father's age. But as I read and reread Dad's memoir, it became apparent that he had assumed many of the parental responsibilities of an eldest child during the family's emigration to northern Alberta. In some regards, I and my siblings were his second family.

As I recall from my childhood, Dad worked a nine-hour day as a carpenter from Monday through Friday and four hours on Saturday building bungalow houses mounted on skids. People within a hundred-mile area around Tofield could buy the houses and have them moved to a basement on their property towed by a truck with "wide load" emblazoned on the back. These houses were built with integrity, determination and twice the number of nails that some contractors used in their hastily constructed houses. Complete with insulation, interior walls and ceilings finished with gyprock, windows, and new shingles—everything but paint and furniture—they always arrived entirely intact without a crack in the "plaster board." (See box below.)

That, too, is how my father and my mother built their lives in Canada. Solidly—with integrity—buttressed by a huge amount of humility, love, and trust—trust in God and in the good will of the people with whom they worked during the week and prayed with on Sundays. There was also a trust that their children would try to do what was right without being *told* what was right. In fact, I can hardly remember any times when I was told how to live, with whom to associate, or what to believe. Our parents' mode of teaching was almost entirely by example. Although they seemed to me to be walking through life with one foot in the 20th century while the other foot trod a path worn by habits of the late 19th century, the values they shared are as relevant for us today as they were when they were born into an idyllic life in the Molotschna Colony near the Sea of Azov, then part of the Russian Empire.

It was the summer of 1976 when Mom and Dad spent a few weeks with me and Betts (Elizabeth Peters, my first wife) in Detmold, West Germany, where we were students at the Nordwestdeutsche Musikakademie. One day

---

Dad's pay was not much above minimum wage. When I asked why he didn't earn a much higher wage as a highly skilled carpenter, he said that Charlie Kallal, his employer, always found steady work for him. Thus, he was able to provide a steady income for our family even during times when others were being laid off from their jobs. Charlie also allowed Dad to take time off for any church work or travel for meetings and conferences that might conflict with his work as a carpenter. Dad was grateful to Charlie as he saw this as a mutually beneficial relationship.

I said to Dad, "Let's go over to the Freilichtsmuseum (outdoor museum) and see what Detmold was like in the past." "*Ja, das können wir*" was his quiet reply. Yes, we could. Dad was a man of few words—except when he stood behind a pulpit in the church in Tofield. (As a child, Dad usually spoke to me in German, and I replied in English. These were the languages in which we comfortably lived our separate lives.) That day I was given a glimpse of the life my parents had left in their youth, the time and the world that had forged their character and their way of life.

As we spent the afternoon in the outdoor museum, I began to understand how my father came to be the man who he was. Born in 1905 under the Tzarist regime in the Russian Empire, his formative years were molded by a nineteenth-century lifestyle in a closed community of Russian Mennonites located near the Molotchna River that flows into the Sea of Azov. (The Sea of Azov lies on the north-east coast of the Crimean Peninsula and flows into the Black Sea through the narrow Kerch Strait.) How could I possibly expect him to understand my life in Germany, a foreign land, a land from where his ancestors came almost 200 years ago? A land where making music was a passion—and, perhaps, a profession for me, some day. He did say, "I tink you haf a good life here." That was high praise from my father; perhaps the first time I heard a hint of affirmation for who and what I aspired to be, especially when he would sometimes say to me, as a child, "*Du bist ein nuisance.*" ("You are a nuisance" were probably the kindest words my father could have used for me when I was a bothersome, obstreperous kid.) But "I tink you haf a good life," even without the limiting word "here," were words that awakened my sense that Dad knew how to be grateful for what I had, even as I had no idea what the future might hold for me. I also gained a new appreciation for the life that my father had lived and for which he was always grateful in spite of the hardships he had endured.

As we wandered through the houses and the barns in the Freilichts-museum, I would occasionally ask the German curators to clarify what a certain item or an outlying building was used for. They often gave vague answers or simply didn't really know the answer. As we walked further on, Dad would quietly tell me about similar implements they had in Russia and for what they were used. Then he would explain what type of work occurred in various buildings or what was stored in a particular outbuilding. I was amazed. This man had grown up on a well-equipped farm in Russia where horses provided the power for transportation and farm work during a time when his father, a progressive farmer, bought his first binder for harvesting grain. After leaving a building, Dad would sometimes quietly add, *"Es war nur größer und besser in Russland."* It was just larger and better in Russia.

That evening, while we were sitting in our living room on woven chairs, Mom crocheting as usual, Dad began to tell stories about his childhood in Russia. That alone was rather unusual. It was Mom who, I recall, would tell us stories about war and famine during her childhood until I began to tune them out. But this evening Dad had funny stories to tell. I recall him telling us about a load of farm goods that he and others from their village of Marienthal took to Berdyansk, a small city on the Sea of Azov. One of the boys, a bit of a blowhard, lay down in the wagon for a nap after they had delivered the farm produce. As he slept soundly, some of the boys quietly secured this boy to the wagon with binder twine. Suddenly they shouted, *"Samson, Samson! Die Philister sind gekommen!"* Every kid knew the biblical story of Samson, how he broke free of the ropes with which the Philistines had tied him in his sleep. But this poor guy couldn't break free when he woke, startled by shouts of "the Philistines are coming." Dad laughed so hard, I though he might slide onto the floor but for his grasp on that armchair. I had never seen him laugh like that. It was so wonderful to see him remember happy childhood times—to see him laugh. We just laughed together with him until we had tears in our eyes, so delighted were we to see him filled with happy memories.

Stories tell us much about who our ancestors were and who we are. Alistair MacLeod describes family stories in *No Great Mischief* when he writes, "One meaning can be true and another can be accurate."[1] There are "truths" and there are facts. (See box on page 8.) Dad usually erred on the side of accuracy—unless he needed God's help with explaining the "truths" necessary to get family members out of Communist Russia on their way to Canada. As I read my father's account of life in Russia, his family's emigration to Canada and his struggle to make a good life for his siblings and his stepmother, it became apparent that he had "a hard life," as Linda has described it. Fortunately, his family did escape the oppressive Soviet regime in 1926 before borders were closed to emigration in 1927. With their arrival in Canada, they escaped an even harder life under Stalin with deportation to Siberia that many of their neighbours endured.

The following document, consisting primarily of Dad's memoir supplemented by his stepmother's diary, tells the story of his family's life in Russia, emigration to Canada, and life in Alberta. It is also one picture (among many) of what it was like to be Mennonite immigrants during the 1920s, to be dedicated Christians, and to be committed members of extended families that helped each other weather the trials of new beginnings. Canada offered them challenges, but also many possibilities for agricultural development; opportunities that were realized through long days of hard work and many sacrifices so that we, the next generation, would have a better life. We, our children, and our grandchildren, are the lucky recipients of wonderful gifts from our parents—the gifts of peace, order, and good government,[2] but also the gifts of faith and principles by which they raised their children and laid the foundation for a good life for us.

To understand the social milieu in which my parents were raised and the land from which they came, it may be helpful to briefly sketch who the Mennonites were and what historical circumstances shaped their lives and their beliefs; what beliefs and circumstances molded the character of individuals within those distinctive people who were Anabaptist Mennonites, often referred to as an ethnic entity.

MacLeod's fictional account of Scots who emigrated to Cape Breton Island echoes the emigration of Mennonites from Russia to the Canadian prairies. Similar to the Scots who spoke Gaelic in Canada, Low German (*Plautdietsch*) was the daily language for most Mennonites as they created a strong support system for each other in their new country. Our parents spoke Low German with each other. However, they spoke in High German to us, their children, while we spoke English, the language we knew best. To my detriment, I heard German spoken at home but didn't learn to speak it properly, so I had to learn to speak High German when I attended the Nordwestdeutsche Musikakademie as a student.

A Brief History of the Early Anabaptists and the Mennonites

One of the leaders of the early Anabaptist Movement was Ulrich Zwingli, a people's priest in Zurich, Switzerland, during the infancy of the early 16th century Protestant Reformation in Europe. Zwingli opposed the corrupt practices of the Catholic hierarchy and sought to make the Gospels available to common people in their own language instead of Latin, the language of the church. Followers of Zwingli such as George Blaurock, Conrad Grebel, and Felix Manz demanded more radical reforms than Zwingli had introduced. This included a renunciation of their own child baptism and being re-baptised based on a personal commitment to follow Jesus. ("Ana" from Greek meaning "again." Hence, Anabaptist.) Abolishing celibacy for the priesthood, embracing high moral standards, and striving to live a life that mirrored the teachings of Jesus were also priorities for this small group of dissidents. There were some early radical Anabaptists such as Thomas Müntzer who urged Martin Luther, the most prominent leader of the Reformation, to give more attention to issues of social justice in accordance with the teachings of Jesus. He gained a large following among the peasants of the southern German states that then engaged in an uprising against the oppression of the nobility. On May 15, 1525, thousands of peasants were killed by the well-armed nobility and Müntzer was captured, tortured, and executed.[3]

In contrast, Anabaptists renounced violence entirely while seeking to live by the words quoted from the *Sermon on the Mount* in Matthew's gospel where Jesus says, "You have heard it said, 'Eye for an eye and tooth for a tooth.' But I tell you, do not resist an evil person. If someone strikes you on the right cheek, turn to him the other also." (Matthew 5: 38-39) Thus, Anabaptists refused to participate in any wars or military service as mercenaries for the local aristocracy. The strong support for reforms of religious and political institutions that they drew from peasants, workers, and common people presented a threat to powerful governing bodies and the established state churches, particularly in the southern German states. (See Appendix 1, **Anabaptists as Revolutionaries.** Page 183.)

The Protestant Reformation resulted in each state in the Holy Roman Empire embracing either Catholicism or Lutheranism during the 16th century. (The Holy Roman Empire was neither holy nor an empire, but merely a loose collection of German-speaking states that was dissolved in 1806.) Anabaptists withheld taxes that supported the state church, and they refused to conform to the strict beliefs, tenets, and rituals, such as the Mass, central to core rites of the established Lutheran and Catholic churches. For their radical beliefs, Anabaptists were hated by people who were baptized at infancy into those two major divisions of the Christian faith.

Being an Anabaptist resulted in one's banishment from much of society. During the 16th century, many were sentenced by both spiritual and political authorities to die. As a result of this harsh persecution, early Anabaptists met in secret for their worship services. As the fledgling movement developed, an emphasis on individual commitment to the teachings of Jesus and a life separate from "the world" led its adherents to establish communities in which they could live according to their understanding of the biblical injunction recorded in the Gospel of John, chapter 15, verse 19, where Jesus says, "If you belonged to the world, the world would love you as its own. As it is, you do not belong to the world, but I have chosen you out of the world. That is why the world hates you."[4] A familiar saying among Mennonites is that they were a people who were "*in* the world, but not *of* the world."

There is some evidence that the Mennonite branch of the Anabaptist movement evolved, almost independently, from the teachings of Erasmus, a prominent Dutch philosopher and theologian of the early 16th century. His writings and spirit may have directly or indirectly influenced the thinking and writings of Menno Simons, a priest who lived and taught in Friesland, a northern province of the Netherlands. It was Countess Anna of East Friesland who, in 1545, allowed peaceful Anabaptists, whom she name *Menists* after Menno, to live in her territory.[5]

Hugo Peters takes up the Dutch Anabaptist story in a brief history that forms a backdrop to our parents who became known as "Russian" Mennonites. It begins with the Protestant Reformation during the 16th century in northern Europe.

[There] arose what has been labelled the Radical Reformation; one such stream was the Anabaptist reformers in Switzerland and Holland. The Dutch branch was named after Menno Simons. He had been a serving Catholic priest, also seeking reform. However, his reading of scripture told him that the church needed to separate itself from worldly structures and return to a practice where members, by their words *and lifestyle*, reflected their allegiance to Jesus – *Christi Nachfolger* (followers of Christ). This was expressed by adult baptism, the refusal to bear arms for the state and the refusal to swear oaths— anathema to civil authorities and both the Catholic and Lutheran Church of the day.

By the late 1500s extreme persecution drove the majority of Mennonites out of the Netherlands, mostly to northern Prussia (today Poland), to the Vistula River delta area in the vicinity of Danzig, where they found asylum under the Polish nobility. Here they applied their lowland diking and drainage skills to convert the river delta into highly productive farmland. It was also here that church services began to be conducted in High German, while *Plautdietsch* (Low German) remained the everyday language. As time went on, however, partly the result of German expansionism, Mennonites were increasingly oppressed via vocational restrictions, excessive taxation and demands for military service. This led to a second migration. (See map on page 12 for Mennonite origins and various paths of emigration.)

Russia had come out the victor in the Russo-Turkish war (1768– 1774) and was anxious to reinforce its hold on south Russia and the Crimea, at that time occupied by roving bands of plundering Cossacks and Tatars. So, in 1763, the new Tsarina, Catherine the Great, invited agriculturists from Europe to settle these sparsely settled territories.[6]

During the Russo-Turkish war, the Turks of the Ottoman Empire were driven south of the Black Sea and the Caucasus Mountains into present-day Georgia, separating Russia from Turkey and Armenia. Under Catherine the Great (who came from Saxony-Anhalt, part of the Prussian empire roughly in the region of Berlin, Dresden, and Leipzig) people were invited by the Russian

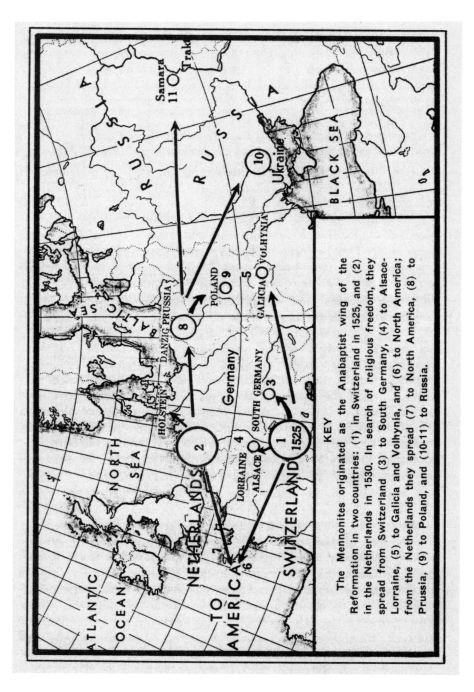

The map contains the following labels and key:

KEY

The Mennonites originated as the Anabaptist wing of the Reformation in two countries: (1) in Switzerland in 1525, and (2) in the Netherlands in 1530. In search of religious freedom, they spread from Switzerland (3) to South Germany, (4) to Alsace-Lorraine, (5) to Galicia and Volhynia, and (6) to North America; from the Netherlands they spread (7) to North America, (8) to Prussia, (9) to Poland, and (10-11) to Russia.

Mennonite Origins and Emigrations

government to colonize these purported "empty lands." These invitations were also extended to people from other German states plus England, Scotland, Denmark, Sweden, Austria and Holland by colonization agents sent by the Russian government.

From 1764 to 1767 more than 100 colonies were established in Russia, mainly by Germanic peoples. However, during a Russian peasant revolt (1772-1774), seventeen colonies were completely destroyed, and thousands of people were killed or sent to Siberia. Yet many Lutherans and Catholics, as well as Mennonites from the Germanic states, continued to arrive during the following century. By 1914, at the beginning of the First World War, there were an estimated two million people of Germanic descent in the Russian Empire. Among them were several very prosperous Mennonite colonies. Chortiza, the "Old Colony," was the first colony established on the Dnieper River in 1789.[7] (See map of the Mennonite colonies in South Russia on page 14.)

Hugo Peters continues his story of the Mennonites with the following observations.

Many Germans responded to [Catherine the Great's] invitation, among them large numbers of Mennonites from [the Danzig area in] Prussia who were promised all the religious freedoms they sought and given large tracts of land specifically reserved for their use. The Chortiza Colony was the first settlement, established in 1789. As a result of continuing in-migration there was pressure to acquire more land; the Mennonites were offered a further land grant in 1803 which became the Molotschna Colony.

Families were large and, while some achieved great prosperity, there were also many not so well off, who often survived as labourers on the larger estates. In 1836, upon request, the Russian government opened a further tract of land for Mennonite settlement. In the next 20 years 149 landless families (read *poor, less educated, less progressive*) from the older colonies were selected to establish the Bergthaler Colony.

No more than 30 years later the Russian government was inclined to gently erode the "privilegium" extended to the Mennonites by

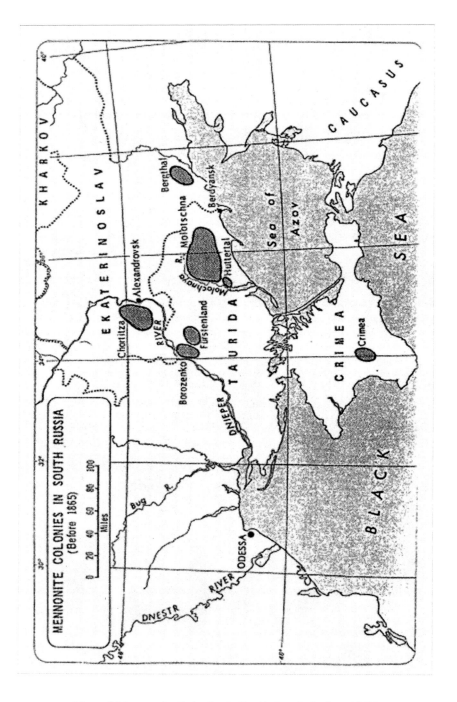

Map of Mennonite Colonies in South Russia before 1865

14

Catherine back in 1789. One dimension of this policy was to pressure them to either accept basic military training or, at the least, some type of alternative service. Church leadership in the (more conservative) Bergthaler Colony immediately perceived this as a betrayal and a serious threat to their religious freedom.[8]

In 1871 (one year after the province [of Manitoba] was established) scouts were sent to Canada. Interestingly, in a repeat of 1789 Russia, the Canadian government, anxious to forestall American intrusion into the West, was most willing to offer land grants and all the promises (privilegium) originally offered by Catherine [the Great]. Another curious parallel was that in those land grant areas lived nomadic peoples called "Indians."[9]

From approximately 9000 individuals who had originally immigrated to Russia, the Mennonite population had increased five-fold to about 45,000 by 1870, mostly in the Chortitza and Molotschna settlements. By 1914 forty daughter colonies were established occupying nearly 12,000 square kilometres (4,600 square miles), with a total population over 100,000.[10]

Historian David Rempel adds details to the picture of Mennonite colonization in the Russian empire during the 18th and 19th centuries. He writes the following in *A Mennonite Family in Tsarist Russia and the Soviet Union, 1789 – 1983*.

[In 1786] Catherine the Great, recognizing the need to populate her newly seized southern territories with industrious families, had sent a recruiting agent to Danzig to entice Mennonites to settle in this virgin land, then called New Russia. Catherine was keenly aware of the Mennonites' aptitudes in farming, dairying, business, and crafts, and likewise cognizant of their dissatisfaction with the discriminatory measures increasingly imposed on them by the Danzig and Prussian authorities. Among the most nettling was a series of special taxes, restrictions on establishing various businesses, and a prohibition on purchasing land except from another Mennonite. In other words, Mennonites in Danzig could never increase their landholdings or provide land for their offspring except at the expense of other

Mennonites. To be sure, these measures did not affect their religious beliefs directly. However, Mennonites could obtain relief only if they compromised their positions. For example, a Mennonite could gain exemption from special taxes if he rendered military service. Or he could buy land if he gave up his membership in the church. For many Mennonites the only ways out were to compromise their religious beliefs or to emigrate. Thus, they were ripe for Catherine's invitation.[11]

Terms of Catherine the Great's Recruiting Manifesto of 1785

1. Free transportation and board from the Russian border to the settlement area.
2. The right to settle anywhere and pursue any occupation.
3. Loans to build houses and factories, or purchase farm equipment.
4. **Perpetual exemption from military and civil service.**
5. Tax exemption for periods that varied with occupation and place of settlement.
6. **Freedom of religion,** except to establish monasteries.
7. The right to proselytize among the Muslims, but not among Christian subjects.
8. The right of self-government in agricultural communities.
9. The right to import family belongings duty-free.
10. The right to buy serfs and peasants for those who established factories with their own money.
11. The right to negotiate other terms with Russian authorities.[12]

Although the terms shown in **bold** were perhaps the main reasons for emigration to Russia, the other terms proved to be very important for the establishment of self-governing social units that encouraged settlers to develop the land acquired from the Ottoman Empire in the Russo-Turkish War of 1768–1774.

In *No Permanent City: Stories from Mennonite History and Life*, Harry Loewen writes about the difficulties the first Mennonites encountered as they settled east of the Dnieper River.

When the First Prussian Mennonites migrated to South Russian in 1789, the question was whether the group would establish compact villages or settle individually on separate pieces of land. Many favored individual farmsteads, for this was how they had lived in Prussia for many centuries.

Jacob Höppner, one of the two deputies and leaders of the Khortitza Mennonites, built his house in the so-called cherry orchard near the Dnieper River, some distance from the nearest farmers. Others did the same. They soon discovered, however, that living far apart from each other was not such a good idea. The defenseless Mennonites were often molested by lawless elements from among the native population in those early years.[13]

In response to the repeated threat of marauders, the Mennonite settlers banded together in villages that afforded them comfort and some protection. The religious, economic, and cultural cohesion of the people in these villages contributed to a rural lifestyle that promoted a prosperity far greater than that of the surrounding indigenous population.

The Russian government did not receive the industrious Mennonites for humanitarian reasons, but because it needed settlers to populate the vast steppes in the south. Moreover, the Mennonites were to become model farmers who would be good examples for others in agriculture, education, and industry.

With skill, intelligence, and great effort, Cornies did all he could to make the Mennonite colonies model communities (see box below). Sheep and cattle were imported from abroad. New stock and breeds were developed. New strains of grain were adapted to south-Russian

---

An Agricultural Society was established with Johann Cornies, a wealthy Mennonite estate owner, as its chairman for life. He contributed much to the success of the early colonies but there were those who opposed him and viewed him as an agent of the government more than an agent of the colonies.

growing conditions. Forests and orchards were planted, an undertaking which eventually made the southern Ukraine a near paradise.[14]

By the early 1900s the Mennonite colonies in Russia had become the most prosperous and well-developed rural communities in all of Russia. For half a century they had been the prize exhibits of Russian colonization officials. Well-planned villages with brick structures, painted fences, flower gardens, rolling fields of grain, millions of cattle and sheep, and expanding industries were indeed a joy to behold. Schools, welfare institutions, and church life were at the height of their development. But at the same time, insecurity in state and society was also approaching its peak. Planned and unplanned Russification was slowly but surely undermining their traditional way of life.[15]

Under the terms of the *Privilegium* promised by Catherine the Great and formalized under her successor, Tsar Paul I, a large measure of autonomy was granted to the Mennonites that included the right to self-governing structures. Only in rare cases were Russian government law enforcement agencies called upon to intervene where serious crimes or raids by local nomads required the strong arm of the law. Referring to themselves as *die Stillen im Land*, the silent ones in the Land, Mennonites avoided political controversy and actions that might draw attention to their way of life or social structures.[16]

Statistics from the 1920s paint a picture of prosperity that eventually put the Mennonites at odds with the Bolshevik revolution. Cornelius (C. J.) Dyck gives a concise overview of the success that the Mennonite colonies achieved by the early 20th century. From the following description, one can see that the Mennonites in "Russia" (Ukraine) had achieved a remarkably high level of comfort and economic security during the 19th century, a standard of living that could be described as a well-to-do middle-class way of life when about 90% of the Russian population still labored as serfs and peasants for wealthy landowners. Dyck cites some of those statistics from the 1920s documenting the achievements of Mennonites in Russia.

From them it appears that there were 120,000 Mennonites in Russia after World War I, of whom 75,000 lived in Ukraine and 45,000 in

Siberia and other parts of Russia. This does not include the 18,000 who emigrated to North America in the 1870s.

The agricultural development promoted by Johann Cornies also made possible and necessary a limited industrial program. Mennonites concentrated on the production of agricultural machinery and the processing of their own agricultural products. Thus, by the early twentieth century they had seventy large steam-powered flour mills, factories whose combined output included 15,000 mowers and 10,000 plows annually, creameries, and other industrial projects. Six percent of the industrial production in Russia was carried on by the Mennonites. But the vast majority of them were farmers. It has been estimated that the industrial wealth, which accounted for 50 to 75 percent of total Mennonite assets, was in the hands of 2.8 percent of the people. Some of them were very wealthy; they travelled or studied in Europe, read Russian books and magazines and, on occasion, socialized with the elite of Russian society in a variety of cultural settings.[17]

This flourishing economy made possible civic and educational programs unmatched anywhere in the Mennonite world at that time. Mutual aid, homes for the aged, orphanages, hospitals, including a psychiatric hospital, a school for deaf-mutes, a girls' school, and a school of business for young men were only a part of the vast provisions the communities made for their people. By 1914 they had 400 elementary and thirteen secondary or high schools, two teachers' colleges, four trade schools, one Bible school, and negotiations were carried on with the government for permission to establish a seminary. In addition, there were approximately 250 Mennonite students attending higher Russian educational institutions and some fifty in seminaries and universities abroad. It is clear that all of these institutions could not have been supported adequately except by congregations who were experiencing a recovery of their spiritual life and were willing to sacrifice for these causes. This willingness was verified further by their support of some 12,000 Mennonite young men in the forestry and medical corps service during World War I which, in 1917 alone, cost the congregations three million rubles.[18]

A literacy rate of over 90% among Mennonites stood in stark contrast to the Russian people who were landless and governed by a Tzarist Ministry of Education that was hostile to the idea of educating the general populace whose literacy rate was about 15%. With the vast majority of Russian people being peasants and serfs before the 1917 revolution, only the wealthy and the aristocracy had access to education. It is interesting to note that, during the early 20th century, Mennonites in Russia tended to be better educated than those who had emigrated to Manitoba in the 1870s.

Anabaptist Mennonites, through their history, have been "on the move" whenever their way of life or their ability to live by the dictates of their conscience was compromised. A group of Quakers and Mennonites settled in Germantown, north of Philadelphia, as early as 1683 at the invitation of William Penn. While Mennonites from the Prussian free state of Danzig were invited to establish a colony in Russia at the end of the 18th century, other Anabaptists from Switzerland migrated to the "New World," the United States of America. With the Communist Revolution of 1917, Russian Mennonites feared that they would be forced to bear arms for the state and that their education, language and way of life would be severely compromised.

Emigration from Russia had begun among some Mennonite groups in 1870 when the government made military service universal prompting whole villages to emigrate to Canada and the United States. In 1874, fearing the loss of tens of thousands of Russia's most productive farmers, the government agreed that military service could be replaced by non-combatant services based on the terms of the *Privilegium*. The main service was forestry work during peace time, but it also included service in the army medical corps during wartime.[19]

World War I, revolution, and famine convinced many Mennonites to leave all their possessions and the good life in Russia and begin again in Canada, the United States, and places like Paraguay in South America. C. J. Dyck points out that "It is clear that freedom of conscience was central to these migrations, particularly if conscience is defined to include the economic, social, and other conditioning factors which shaped their life together as much as pure religious convictions. And conscience worked differently with different people, urging some to leave for the sake of their faith and some to stay for the same reason."[20]

It was Dad's stepmother's family, the Funks, who decided that emigrating to Canada was a wise choice after the Russian Revolution and a famine in the 1920s. Dad was somewhat ambivalent about leaving Russia, but Grandma Barbara's family insisted that she and her children should emigrate. In retrospect, Dad saw the decision to leave all behind and begin a new life as God's will for him and his family.

Edgar Rogalski, son of Anna (Neufeld) Rogalski, Dad's sister, writes about the Neufelds in his introduction to a very brief diary written by Dad's father titled *Diary of Johann Neufeld and Barbara Funk Neufeld: From the Russian Revolution to Pioneer Life in Peace River, Alberta*. There he elaborates on the changing conditions in the Mennonite colonies that prompted the emigration of the Neufeld family to Canada. ("The Funks" refers to Dad's stepmother Barbara Funk's family. She was the daughter of Gerhard Funk and Aganetha [Voth] Funk. Barbara was Dad's father's third wife, the first two having died shortly after childbirth.)

The Funks and Neufelds settled in Molotschna, in Mariawohl and Marienthal respectively. When the Russian Empire under Tsar Alexander II tried to Russify the German-speaking colonies in the early 1870s, some 20,000 Mennonites left for Canada and the United States. The majority, however, adapted to the new rules concerning Russian language education. They accepted an alternative to military service by planting trees (*Forsteidienst*) on the treeless prairie of the Ukraine. The growing industrialization in Western Europe and the development of railways increased the demand for grain from the Ukraine which was sometimes referred to as the "breadbasket of Europe." The Mennonite colonists proved to be successful farmers and their prosperity allowed them to develop a booming manufacturing industry and a complex infrastructure of schools, churches, health care, municipal government, and a host of craft industries. *Forever*

Summer, Forever Sunday, [a photobook by Peter Gerhard Rempel] reflects some of the idyllic and comfortable life enjoyed by the Mennonite minority which numbered about 150,000 at the beginning of the First World War. The Mennonite Commonwealth, as it was sometimes called, was spread all over the Ukraine and reached into Western Siberia and the regions of Kazakstan.

With the advent of the First World War (1914–1918) the Mennonites suddenly became hated German foreigners. With the disastrous defeat of the Russian armies at the hand of the advancing German forces, Russia fell apart. The Mennonite world was subsequently shattered by civil war, anarchist destruction, disease, and famine. The new triumphant Bolshevik government was intent on ending privilege, private property, and faith in God. This affected the Neufeld family in a profound way. The Mennonites were suspected of being collaborators with the occupying German forces and of supporting the old Tsarist regime in the civil war between the White Russian army and the Red Russian army. The German army had briefly occupied the Ukraine after the Treaty of Brest-Litovsk in March 1918. Less than a year later Germany withdrew, but German soldiers left guns in the Mennonite villages so that the villagers could defend themselves from the ensuing chaos and lawlessness that was about to descend upon the undefended colonists. Weapons of any kind went against the non-resistant teaching of the German-speaking Mennonites. The new Bolshevik government demanded that each village surrender six guns to communist officials. Failure to produce the often-non-existent guns from villagers who had refused to arm themselves meant prison and execution.

Johann Neufeld spent six weeks imprisoned in an overcrowded, unsanitary cellar when he failed to produce a gun. Many prisoners were called out and were shot to death. Johann escaped this fate, but he had contracted tuberculosis and died in January 1924. Johann's distaste for the Bolsheviks had already led him to withdraw his children from school when he objected to the teaching of atheism in the school curriculum. My mother, Anna, recalls standing, looking longingly out the window watching the other children on their way to school. Although Johann died before he could bring his family to Canada, his dying wish was that the family leave as soon as possible.

In the early 1920s Canada offered a ray of hope to some 20,000 Mennonites as a land of freedom and opportunity to rebuild their shattered lives. The Neufeld/Funk family and many of their relatives were able to leave their old beloved homeland and make a new home in Canada. Stalin slammed the door on any further emigration from Russia in 1927. Those Mennonites who chose to remain, or who were not permitted to leave, suffered unspeakable horrors in the years to come.[21]

In 1919, an Order-in-Council passed by the Canadian Government under Prime Minister Sir Robert Borden prohibited Doukhobors, Hutterites, and Mennonites from immigration into Canada. It stated that, "owing to their peculiar customs, habits, modes of living, and methods of holding property, they are not likely to become assimilated or to assume the responsibilities of Canadian citizenship within a reasonable period of time." Contributing to this commonly held perception were various groups on the Canadian prairies that were hostile to the Mennonites because they spoke German and because of the pacifism that exempted them from military service during the First World War. Additionally, Russia was on a list of undesirable East European countries from which immigration was excluded. David Toews, a schoolteacher and church elder in Saskatchewan, played a major role in arranging for thousands of Mennonites to emigrate to Canada despite the obstacles presented by the government.

There was also some resistance from Mennonites already in Canada who feared that the guarantees they were required to provide for incoming Mennonites would lead to their financial ruin. Some even believed that the years of suffering visited on the "*Russlaender*" were due to their prosperity, worldliness, and lack of spirituality.

In 1921, Prime Minister William Lyon Mackenzie King who had grown up near Mennonites in Waterloo County, Ontario, became prime minister. After meeting with a delegation of Mennonites in June of 1922 the new Liberal government revoked the 1919 Order-in-Council prohibiting Mennonite immigration. Toews, in a letter of appreciation to the prime minister, aptly expressed the sentiments of our parents and those who arrived in Canada in the 1920s.[22]

> It is with the deepest feeling of appreciation that all our Mennonite people have read the glad news that the Order-in-Council prohibiting Mennonite immigration has been repealed.... We are again on a level with others with whom we will gladly co-operate in service to Canada which we learned to love as our home... and I hope that we, our children, and others of our stock who may yet settle in this our beloved Canada may ever prove worthy of the confidence you place in us.[23]

It is with deep gratitude that we recognize the courage of our parents and their families as they decided to sell all they possessed in Russia to finance the journey to an unknown future in a cold, unfamiliar climate in western Canada. While most of their neighbours remained in Russia hoping for a better future, they secured our place among the most fortunate people in the world by beginning a new life in Canada equipped with virtually nothing more than determination and a willingness to work hard. It is with deep sorrow that one contemplates the lot of the approximately 80,000 Russian Mennonites who chose not to emigrate or were not permitted to leave Russia. Most of them were destined to experience the horrors of dispossession, deportation and, for many, annihilation under Stalin's dictatorial Communist regime.

Genealogical Background of the Johann Neufeld Family

Neufeld is not an uncommon name in the regions of Berlin and Brandenburg in northeastern Germany even today. The name literally means "new field," perhaps originally assigned to or taken by someone who was the guy with the new field. Or the name was given to "settlers" who moved to newly reclaimed land won either by draining marshes or by pushing back the sea in the coastal lands with river marshes and estuaries from Flanders in northern Belgium to Danzig in northern Poland. Often, people took surnames descriptive of their new location, names like Neudorf (new village) and Neustadt (new town) as well as Neufeld. In the Vistula delta (West Prussia), the Mennonite name of Neufeld (or its Low German form, Niefelt) appeared as early as 1600."[24]

The first record of our Neufeld ancestors locates them in Klein Lichtenau near Danzig. Gehrt Neufeld was born in Klein Lichtenau in about 1728 (d. 1798) in what was Polish Prussia. He married Anna Dircksen who was born in Heubuden, Prussia, in about 1735 (d. 1812). (See box below.)

> The 1776 Prussian census lists nine Mennonite families in Klein Lichtenau with the following surnames: Barckmann, Claassen, Friesen, Mattis, Neyfeldt, Penner, and Toews. In 1820, the village had 341 residents, including 44 Mennonites. Mennonites who were residents of Klein Lichtenau were members of the Heubuden Mennonite Church.[25]

Gehrt Neufeld's son, Gehrt, born in Danzig-Heubuden in 1760, married Catharina Conrath in 1788. She was born in 1759 in Neuendorf near Danzig. Their son, Gerhard, was born on October 28, 1795, in Danzig-Stadtgebiet and married Anganetha Thiessen on July 16, 1828. She was born in about 1796, also in Prussia. Gerhard and Anganetha's son, Johann, Dad's grandfather, was born on September 16, 1833, in Marienburg in what was Gross Preußen or West Prussia. As a six-year-old child, he emigrated with his parents to the South Russian Mennonite colony of Molotschna and settled in the village of Elisabetthal. There he married Katharina Wiens from the nearby village of Pordenau in 1858. She was born on January 24, 1839. Soon after the wedding they bought a farm on the north side of the village of Marienthal.

Helmut T. Huebert gives an account of Marienthal's history in *Molotschna Historical Atlas* of which the following is an excerpt. (See map on page 27.)

> Marienthal was founded in 1820 in the southeast corner of the Molotschna Colony. The village was laid out along the Tschokrak River,

---

A genealogy, created by Edgar Rogalski shows the lineage of today's Neufeld family going back to the early 18th century.

which at that location must have been only a rivulet. The land was flat and had very little topsoil. Hay yield was meager, but cereal crops did well. The land had originally been rented by Johann Cornies, then sublet to Nogai nomads as pasture.

Specific plots were designated by ploughing the borders and the site for each farmer decided by lot. The first spring the families built wooden or sod huts, then did the planting, after which they constructed their houses. Marienthal survived many adversities in the first years. About 80% of the farmers had horses stolen making farm work rather difficult. In 1823 grasshoppers destroyed the crops. The meagre crop of 1824 was followed by terrible winter storms during which most of the cattle perished. In 1825 hail flattened the crops. Marienthal suffered severely in the great drought year of 1833. On January 11, 1838, an earthquake caused a number of deep wells (35 to 45 feet) to collapse. The all-pervasive east wind caused considerable damage; in 1842, for example, much of the seeded grain and topsoil was blown away. [Dad's father and grandparents arrived in 1839.]

In 1908 the population of Marienthal was 444 living on 1760 dessiatines. [One dessiatine, a measurement used in Tzarist Russia, was equal to about 2.7 acres or 1.09 hectares.][26]

Dad's memoir gives an account of life in Marienthal during his youth until his family emigrated in 1926. (He was born in 1905). During the latter years, before they left Marienthal, the people in the village experienced hardship and suffering due to the civil war and famine that followed the Russian Revolution of 1917. The layout of the village in 1941 shows that there were still 56 Mennonite families living in Marienthal. (See page 28.) Similarly, the layout of Pordenau in the late 1920s shows 52 names of people living there after the Enns family, Mom's family, left. (See page 29.) It is interesting to note the absence of the Enns name on the Pordenau map and, similarly, the absence of the Neufeld name on the map of Marienthal.

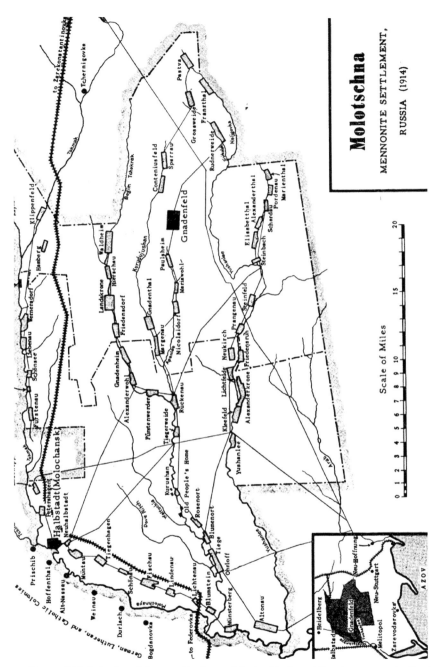

Map of Molotschna Mennonite Area. Marienthal and Pordenau are in the lower right of the map. Lines show roads and paths and a jagged line shows the railway.

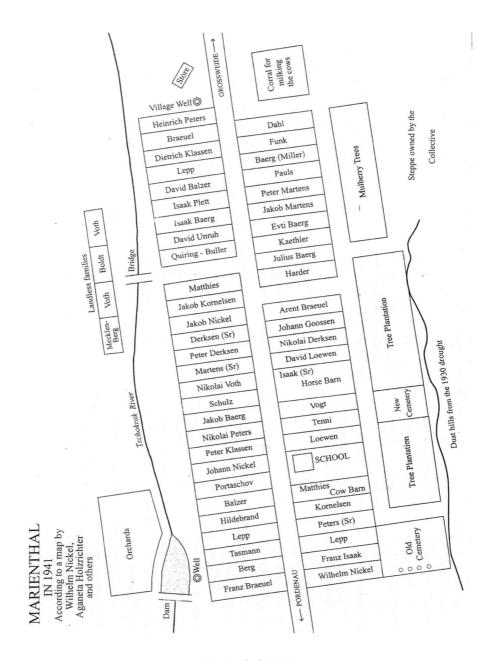

Marienthal 1941

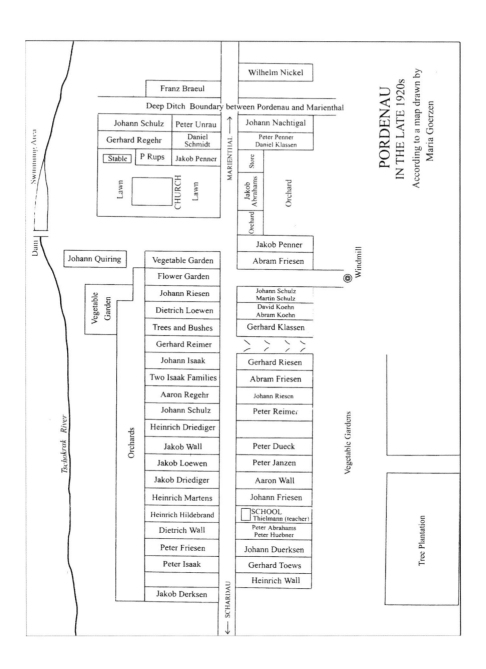

Pordenau in the late 1920s

Helmut Huebert writes the following about Pordenau in *Molotschna Historical Atlas*.

When emigration to Canada became a possibility, there does not seem to have been great interest. Only ten family groups... are listed as leaving from Pordenau. In the early 1930s Pordenau suffered the same atrocities as other villages in the Molotschna. At least nine families were forced off their land as kulaks. (See box below.) The Walls moved to Rudnerweide, a Reimer and a Schulz family were sent to the far east (Siberia) and starved to death. Most of the others actually stayed in the village, but not in their homes. In 1930 the population of the village was 332; by 1936 it was down to 250. At least 16 men were arrested in the 1930s, and eight were drafted into the Red Army.

After the church was closed in 1933 the building was used as a club, theatre, movie house and dance hall.[27] (See photos on p.31.)

In 1941, during the approach of the German army, most of the population of Pordenau was *verschleppt* (sent into exile). Without the insistence of John Enns, Mom's eldest brother, her family would likely not have emigrated to Canada in 1926. Her father had been reluctant to leave the village and the beautiful environs where they lived. However, during his years performing alternate service for the Russian government, John kept writing letters insisting that the family must leave as soon as possible. Sadly, he died of starvation in the 1930s, exiled from his Molotschna homeland.

After the German invasion of June 1941, able-bodied men and women from the village of Marienthal were forced to dig trenches and tank traps near the Dnieper River for the Russian military. The remaining men aged 16-65 were sent 1200 kilometres by foot to be put on freight trains and shipped north and east. Of 57 people who were deported in September, two were brothers by

---

Kulak (Russian: for "fist"). in Russian and Soviet history, a wealthy or prosperous peasant, generally characterized as one who owned a relatively large farm and several head of cattle and horses and who was financially capable of employing hired labour and leasing land. Before the Russian Revolution of 1917, the kulaks were major figures in the peasant villages. They often lent money, provided mortgages, and played central roles in the villages' social and administrative affairs.[28]

*Louise, my mother, wrote on the photo, "The church I went to as a little girl.
My dad in white jacket and Johan Rups who worked for my dad for 36 years."*

*Pordenau Mennonite Sunday School class. Mom sits in the front row,
3rd from the right, with a little check mark on her white dress.*

the name of Nickel. When the Germans retreated in 1943, the entire village of Marienthal was destroyed by fire.[29]

In 1976, when my parents came to visit my wife and me in Germany, we took them to Pforzheim to meet Mr. and Mrs. Nickel who had recently emigrated to Germany from Siberia in their retirement. (In the 1970s it was common for the Soviets to "repatriate" old people of German descent to West Germany.) It was 50 years since Dad last saw them when his family emigrated to Canada in 1926. Nickel and his beautiful young wife had remained in Russia believing that times would be good again, ignoring the warnings that prompted most Mennonites to emigrate. Mr. Nickel's description of his family's journey to Siberia and their life in that bleak land was unimaginable. It was a very hard life. Only one of their four children survived. Yet, through all their tribulations, they had learned to be grateful for life's simplest gifts as they now lived in their tiny two-room apartment in Germany. Was this, perhaps, the Nickel that Huebert refers to when he writes, "A number of Marienthal villagers have now moved to Germany as *Aussiedler*? Among these are Wilhelm Nickel, Aganeta Holzrichter, Margaretha Isaak, Elisabeth Klett and Anna Boldt."[30] (*Aussiedler*—an evacuee or emigrant.) Citizens of the Soviet Union who were of German descent and of retirement age were strongly encouraged to emigrate during the 1970s. West Germany accepted them, providing them with a small two-room apartment and enough amenities and social services to live in comfort relative to what they had endured in Siberia.

Dad remembered Nickel as being a rather headstrong young man, but he now was a humble, bent figure with only three remaining teeth of which he was very proud and a shrunken wife, stooped and wrinkled by decades of hard labour. As Mom and Dad sat down for a "dinner" of noodles, broth, and a small loaf of dark rye bread with Nickel and his wife, Nickel gave thanks to God for the food and the many blessings in his life. Then, he broke the loaf into four equal pieces, giving each of the four elderly people at the table one piece. With elbows on the table, he and his wife bent over their food as they savored the meagre meal in total silence. When they were done, Nickel said to Dad, "See how we live like royalty in this country?" I have never seen anyone eat with such gratitude and be so grateful for the very few possessions in their tiny two-room apartment.

I am reminded of cold wintery mornings in our little house in Tofield, Alberta. Before wolfing down our breakfast and running off to school, Dad would devote a good deal of time during his pre-breakfast prayer to giving thanks for all the "riches" in our lives and for the peaceful country in which we live.

John Neufeld's Memoir

Linda tells me that Dad wrote his memoir, *Was ich gesehen, gehört und erlebt habe*, (*What I Have Seen, Heard and Experienced*) in 1977 during times when Mom was away from home busily preparing food for Meals on Wheels in Calgary. He had time to reflect on his past. His writing style and his sentences often have an element of stream of consciousness as they flow along the lines of many pages with very few changes or edits. Reading the original in German, one experiences the style and nuance with which Mennonites spoke *Hochdeutsch*, high German. Over a century of living in Russia, mostly isolated from German culture, Mennonite German had a noticeable accent and a nuance that differed quite markedly from the "proper German" I heard while studying at a music academy in Northern Germany from 1973 to 1977. One can still hear a variety of accents and dialects throughout present-day Germany, so it is not surprising that Mennonites, living in rather closed "colonies" in Russia, would have developed their own nuances with spoken German.

So, who was Johann (John) Neufeld, often referred to by his birth family as Hans (see box below) and by Mom as *Hohns* in *Plautdietsch*, Low German, the everyday language of Mennonites? And what does his story tell us about who we are? John Neufeld's memoir begins with the story of how the Neufeld family emigrated from the Danzig area in Prussia (now Gdansk, Poland) to live in the Russian Empire under Tzarist rule.

"Hans" is the short form for Johann in German. High German was the language of church and school among Russian Mennonites.

I have included brief explanations of various historical events in my father's memoir as well as memories that I, or others, have of our parents' oral history. Although Dad seldom reminisced about "the good ol' days" in Russia or of deprivation and terror after the 1917 revolution, it was Mom who spoke more often about the memories engrained in her mind as a child before emigrating to Canada at the age of 10. I have interspersed selections from the diary of Dad's stepmother that she began following the death of her husband, Johann (Dad's father), in 1924. Her first entry begins;

> *Our beloved Papa died on January 24th at 4:00 am. The funeral and burial took place on January 30. Johann Neufeld of Marienthal reached the age of 55 years, 4 months, and 10 days. The funeral sermon was given by Johann Martens based on John 12:24, "Truly, I tell you unless a grain of wheat falls into the earth and dies, it remains a single grain; but if it dies, it bears much fruit."*

Barbara Neufeld's diary then continues from June 1926 giving her view of what life was like for members of the family during emigration and during the time when they struggled to create a new life in Canada.

In the following narrative, I have omitted some of Dad's descriptions of many ancestors of the Neufeld and Enns families. They can be found in the original German manuscript or the English translation where Dad carefully lists the dates of birth, marriage, and death that he remembered at the time of writing. However, you will find some of his relatives and their children listed in the following narrative, particularly those in Russia. The descriptions that are included provide an insight into the lives of those people and the ever-present reality of an early death.

Pages 124 -129 and 137 -140 list Mom and Dad's siblings and their children. However, Dad omitted his own children, presumably because we knew the details of our families in 1977. Mom and Dad's descendants in 2022 have been included on pages 158 to 176.

You will see three different fonts used to distinguish the sources in the following narrative. The **bold print** gives the reader the option to read John Neufeld's memoir without interruption. In *italics* one can read the interpolations from his stepmother's diary written during and after emigration.

In this font that you are now reading are comments and recollections by me, Gerald Neufeld. They are inserted as further explanations of historical events that Dad refers to as well as my memories of conversations with my parents and some personal observations of their character and lived experiences. You will also see boxes at the bottom of some pages for brief explanations of the text. Endnotes are included as source citations at the end of the book.

- **Johann (John) Neufeld's memoir**.
- *Barbara (Funk) Neufeld's diary, (John Neufeld's stepmother)*.
- Comments and recollections by Gerald Neufeld, fourth child of John and Louise Neufeld.

What I Have Seen, Heard and Experienced by John Neufeld

Written in German in 1977 in Calgary, Alberta.
This English version is based on a translation by Linda Neufeld

Neufeld Family in Russia: Early Years

Grandfather Johann Gerhard Neufeld was born on August 31, 1833, in Prussia (Germany). When he was six years old, in the year 1839, his parents, he, and his brother, who was somewhat younger than he was, emigrated to Russia. In the days of his old age, he told me that he could remember the house in which they had lived and also had some memories of the long journey that had been made with horses and a wagon.

In Russia they came to the Molotschna Mennonite settlement. The village of Eliesabetthal is where they stayed the first while. Perhaps his parents had relatives in that village. The villages of Marienthal, Pordenau, Schardau and Alexandertal were settled already in 1820. The settlement of Eliesabetthal began in 1824.

Soon after moving, grandfather's father (Gerhard Neufeld, born October 28, 1795) bought farm No. 10 in the village of Marienthal which, during my time, belonged to Johan Martens. In the next village of Pordenau, a church had been built and so it was called the Pordenau Mennonite Church. Here grandfather and his brother were baptized and became members of that congregation.

When grandfather was twenty-five years old, he married Katarina Wiens who was probably from the village of Pordenau. Katarina Wiens, our grandmother, was born on January 24, 1839. (June 24, 1839, according to Johann Neufeld, Dad's father's diary.) **Soon thereafter grandfather bought farm No. 5 on the north side of the street in the village of Marienthal. His brother Gerhard bought or took over the farm which his father had. I can remember seeing grandfather's brother as an old man over seventy-five years of age in that house.**

Because grandfather could sing well and loved to sing, he was soon elected as *Vorsänger* (song leader) in the Pordenau Church—that is, he had to announce the hymns to be sung. When he was forty-one years old, in 1874, he was called to be a minister in the Pordenau Church. He served as minister in that congregation for over 35 years. He was not a learned man but, as others have told me, he was a very highly respected and beloved minister. During my time, or during the time of which I can remember, I had not heard him preach. He was already too old, but I have seen him sit—every Sunday—where the ministers sat in the church.

The Lord gave grandfather and grandmother six children. I will write of them as much as I heard and saw.

 Katarina was the oldest daughter. Father's sister was six years older than he. She was born on January 24, 1862 (see top box on p 37). When she was twenty-two years old, on May 27, 1884, she married Peter Goerz. He was the neighbour's son. He was a teacher for a number of years in a Mennonite village in the Crimean Peninsula. In the year 1890, when the Molotschna Colony bought land for the landless and founded twelve villages in the **Province of Samara** (see middle box on p 37), **the Peter Goerzes** (see bottom box on p 37) **went there.**

Dad's father's family.
Left to right. Maria (1870-1915), Gerhard (1872-1926), Katherine (1839-1909), Johann (Dad's father, 1868-1924), Johann Gerhard (Dad's grandfather, 1833-1923), Aganeta (1874-1898). Absent: Katarina (1862-1924)

An entry in the diary of Johann Neufeld (Dad's father) states, "My sister Katharina was born on the 8th of February 1862." (Not January 24th).[31]

Samara is located on the Volga River about 1500 kms north-east of the Molotschna region.

Families were often referred to by the father's first name plus the plural of the family name. Thus, the family of Peter Goerz was called "the Peter Goerzes" rather than Peter Goerz's family. This mode of speech was probably used to distinguish a specific family from many other families with the same surname. My family might have been referred to as "the John Neufelds" to distinguish us from other Neufeld families that lived in and near Tofield.

For a while he taught school there too. Then he gave up teaching, bought a farm in, I think, the village of Podolsk, and became a farmer. The settlement there, however, elected him as "*Waisenman*" (translated literally as "orphan man"), that is, he was to manage the money of orphans until they were twenty-one years old at which time they could receive the same. Here in Podolsk, the Mennonite Brethren congregation had their church. The Peter Goerzes transferred their membership to this Brethren congregation. (See box below.)

The Lord gave them seven children of which I have seen the oldest son Peter and the youngest daughter Sara. Sara worked as a nurse in the mental institution of Betania in the Old Colony. In 1921 she came to visit us.

Peter, the oldest son, I met for the first time in 1938 in Lindbrook (Alberta) to where he and his family had moved. When he was a young man, he wanted to be a missionary. He went to Germany and studied theology in Berlin. Before the advent of World War I, he came home and could not return to Germany to continue his studies. He married Maria Franz. They emigrated to Canada in 1924 or 1925. They farmed at Crowfoot for a number of years. During the '30s when there was a drought, they moved to Lindbrook where he also farmed. Already in Russia he had been called as a minister in the Mennonite Brethren church and here he also laboured much for the Lord. He had a large family, he also had various difficulties with some of his sons. In 1956 his wife died. His second wife was Anna Dick from Pincher Creek. He sold his farm to his son Abe and moved to Edmonton where he lived in his retirement. In 1972, his second wife died. Soon after that he went to St. Catharines, Ontario, to the Manor Senior Citizens Home where I visited him in February 1974. He was 88 years old. He died on May 14, 1976, in St. Catharines and was buried near Tofield (Lindbrook) on May 18.

Due to a lack of ministers and a low level of education among the first Mennonites in Russia before about 1850, there was a perception among some Mennonites that there was a need for a deeper spiritual life. Following a spiritual awakening influenced by the Moravian Brethren and Lutheran Pietists, a small group of Mennonites formed the Mennonite Brethren Church with the objective of leading a more religious life based on the Gospels. Full immersion at baptism became a hallmark of their confession of faith.

Then the second son Herman was a little older than my father. Of him little was said. When I asked Father how it was that there was an age difference of six years between his older sister Katarina and himself, he said there had been a brother, between Katarina and himself, who had drowned as a small boy. Then there was Father—born on September 16, 1868. Of him I will write later.

Father's other sister, Maria, was born on July 3, 1870. On June 6, 1895, she married Abram Heidebrecht from Hamberg. He was a widower who had several children—six or seven—some of whom were grown. As I heard it, he was twenty years older than his second wife. They had three children—Neta, Gerhard and Dietrich. I can remember that they would come home to our place at Christmas and Easter. Abram Heidebrecht suffered badly from asthma. I am not sure which year it was—whether 1916 of 1917—one Sunday when Father and Grandfather returned from church, two men from the village of Hamberg arrived at our home. It was winter and they had come by sled. They said that both Abram Heidebrecht and his wife had died. He had died of asthma around noon, she had had the flu but had arranged the funeral arrangements and she herself died during the night. Father and Grandfather went to the funeral, and I could go along. The funeral was in the house, there stood two coffins, and at the cemetery both coffins were lowered into the one grave.

What was to become of the three children now? The other children of the first wife were already married. Gerhard Neufeld, Father's younger brother who lived in Paulsheim and had a large family, took these three children to live with him.

Then there was his sister Aganeta. She was born on May 14, 1874. She married Peter Voth, also from the village of Hamberg. It was on January 15, 1898 that they had their wedding and on October 8 they had a son, John. She was sick then and died on December 5th. The funeral was on December 9, 1898. Peter Voth married again and lived later in the village of Alexandertal. They had five more children. Because Peter Voth did not own any land (he mainly worked as a labourer) he had John go into higher education in Alexanderkrone, which he also completed. During the revolution he joined the White Army. For quite a while his parents heard nothing of him. During the year 1920 when I attended high school in Alexandertal and had room and board at the Peter Voths, he suddenly came home. He had been captured by the Red Army. When he came home, his clothes were very ragged, and he was full of lice. Great effort was put into cleaning him, but he soon got typhoid fever. He experienced a conversion then and also got his health back. His conversion, however, lacked depth. Soon he was hired as a secretary in the Soviet Office, was then also transferred to the Russian village of Takmak where he also worked as a secretary. Here he met a Jewish girl whom he married. I have heard that he was very much inclined toward Soviet Communistic ideas.

Father's younger brother Gerhard was born on March 4, 1872. He was one who served in the forestry service. He married Maria Friesen of Paulsheim. They had their wedding on January 11, 1901. Since Maria was an only child, after the wedding, Gerhard took over the farm. He was very successful on the farm and as a farmer. The Lord sent them eight children— five sons and three daughters. He very much desired to have his sons go on to further education. In 1926 when we emigrated, he and his family also wanted to emigrate. He had everything ready—the passport, the medical document from the doctor, his farm was also sold. On a designated day they had an auction sale. They had done quite well with the auction. At night, when the family was sleeping, some men—robbers—came. It was August and since it was somewhat warm in the house, Willy, one of the sons, slept outside in front of the door on a bench. The robbers first beat Willy who screamed. His father, Uncle Gerhard Neufeld, heard this, opened the window, and jumped out to help his son. One of the robbers shot him and the bullet went through his chest. The robbers disappeared then without taking any money. The boys drove their father to the hospital in Muntau, but he was dead on arrival.

The funeral was held in a couple of days. Then the sons, with their mother and all the siblings as well as old Grandfather Friesen, emigrated to Canada. Gerhard, one of the sons, had emigrated a few months before this. At first they came to Kitchener, Ontario, then they moved to Vineland,

Ontario. Gerhard had married in Russia. Cornelius, Willy, Peter and Susie married in Ontario. John, Mary and Katie remained single. Soon after their arrival in Canada, old Grandfather Friesen died in Vineland, and then the mother also died a few years later. John, Mary and Katie have always lived together, first on a farm, and when the farm was sold, they retired and lived in Vineland. Cornelius and Gerhard, who also each had a large farm, are also retired. Willy still works on his farm, as also Peter. Susie, who married Peter Dyck, lived near Dunnville, Ontario, on a farm. In February 1974 we were in Ontario and visited all of them.

Now of my father. He was born in the village of Marienthal on September 16, 1868. Here he also went to school. The school at that time was very plain as were also the instructions so that Father did not have very much education. In the Pordenau Church where Grandfather was minister, Father was baptized. At the age of twenty-nine he got to know Helena Bekker from the village of Schardau. As was the custom he had asked his father if he would go to the Bekkers and ask if they would give him Helena to be his wife. Grandfather had gone to the Bekkers and they had consented readily. They had decided that the engagement would be on October 30, 1899, and the wedding on November 12, 1899. Helena Bekker was born on April 7, 1872.

Father took his young wife and lived at Grandfather's in the *Sommerstube* (summer room). I will here describe our house. When we came in the front door we came first in the "*Vorderhaus*" (also *Vorhaus*, fore room), then on the left hand was the summer room and on the right hand the *große Stube* (big room). In the middle of the house there was a wall. From the big room one could go to the *Ekstube* (corner room). This was usually used as a bedroom, whereas the big room was used as a guest room or living room. From the corner room one went into the *kleine Stube* (little room) which was also used as a bedroom and also as a family room. Then one went from the little room into the *Hinterhaus* (back house or room). This was across from the *Vorderhaus* (front house) and the *Sommerstube* (summer room). Between them was the *kleine Küche* (little kitchen) where the cooking and frying occurred. The back room had a door leading outside. Next to the back room were two little pantries, one was the pantry through which one went to the cellar, the other was a chamber in which one kept ham and other meat. From the backroom was a door that led into the barn. The barn was connected to the house.

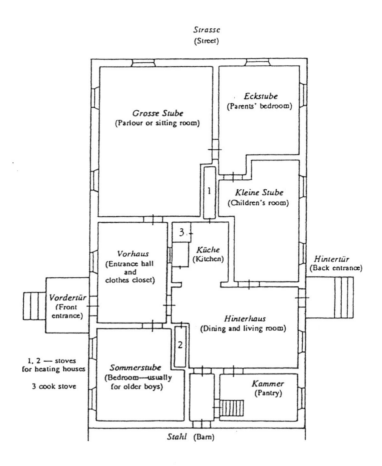

Floor Plan of a Typical Mennonite Home

Father lived, as I have written, with his young wife Helena in the summer room. He worked then on Grandfather's farm.

I will now quote Father's words which he wrote in a book that I can still read. "On the morning of November 13, 1900, my dear Helena became ill and only on November 16 she was delivered in unspeakable pain of a little stillborn son. After that she was so weak that it seemed she would not live to see that evening. She, however, recovered some strength. We have then discussed much, and so after a four-week illness she died peacefully in the belief in her saviour." Thus far, Father's quotation.

Father once told me that in the last hours, when he and his parents had stood at her deathbed and had believed she was already dead, then had she opened her eyes once more, motioned for him to come nearer, and said that she had already seen something very beautiful, something very glorious. She could, however, not describe it with words—it had been far too beautiful. She now wanted to go to that which she had seen and heard. Father said she had seen the heavenly glory. After she had spoken, she died. The funeral was on December 10, 1900.

Four years was Father a widower and then he married Anna Nachtigal. Father once told me how the loving God had led our Mam to him. Once, as his former father-in-law Peter Bekker (Schardau) had visited his brother Heinrich Bekker in the village of Rudnerweide, Heinrich Bekker had asked, "and is Helena's husband, Johann Neufeld married already?" "No," Peter Bekker had said. "Well, he should marry Anna Nachtigal," Heinrich Bekker had said.

Who was Anna Nachtigal? Heinrich Bekker's wife's brother, Peter Nachtigal (Heinrich's brother-in-law), his wife had died. He had three children, Peter, Heinrich and Anna. He (Peter Nachtigal) married again but after a little while he died. His wife, who wanted to marry again, did not, however, want to have these three children (from Peter Nachtigal's first marriage). Where should they now stay? There was no orphanage as was built later in the village of Grossweide. Someone took the two boys along to the Province of Ufa. Anna, however, came to her uncle, Heinrich Nachtigal, who lived in the village of Franztal. Here, however, Anna, our Mama, did not experience parental love. They had a daughter to whom preference was always given. Anna Nachtigal, who was smaller physically, generally had to do the more strenuous work.

When Heinrich Bekker had spoken to Anna Nachtigal on an opportune occasion regarding whether she would be willing to marry a Johann Neufeld, she had been very happy. Peter Bekker, at his convenience, spoke to our Father about this. When Father had then driven to Anna Nachtigal on an occasion, he had known right away that she was the one the Lord had for him. On June 12, 1904, they were engaged and on June 23 they had the wedding. That is how Father and our Mama had met.

Mama was born on February 5, 1881, in the village of Rudnerweide. She was twenty-three years old when she got married, Father was thirty-six years old. Father and Mama again lived in the summer room at Grandfather's. Mama had been a very poor girl but had found a home with Father, and Father and Mama were very happy. Grandfather and Grandmother were also very good to her.

I was born on June 6, 1905, and my sister Maria was born on October 28, 1906. On August 19, 1908, my brother Peter was born. Then on February 26, 1909, Grandmother died after she was a little over seventy years old. I can remember little of Grandmother—only something of the funeral. The funeral was in the house. I was sick and had to stay in bed in the summer room.

Father has written the following in a book, "In October of the year 1907, I drove to the settlement of Samara to visit my sister Katharina, Mrs. Peter Goerz." The reason, however, was not only the visit, but rather he wanted, if possible, to purchase a farm. Until then, Father had only worked for Grandfather. He already had a family, he also wanted to own something. He wanted to buy half of the farm from Grandfather, but Grandfather did not wish this. When Father came back from Samara, Grandfather knew, now was the time. So Father bought half the farm and worked the whole farm—that is, also Grandfather's half.

Father has told us of this trip to Samara. He and three or four other men from our village had gone there. They had gone by train to the station at Sorotchinsk. There they hired a Russian driver who was to take them to the settlement. It took four or five hours to go there by horses. Suddenly, there was a severe blizzard. The horses walked constantly slower. Suddenly the

Johann Neufeld & Anna Nachtigal.
Johann (Hans) b. 1905, Maria b. 1906.
Photo taken in Marienthal, 1907

driver said, "Now we are lost." That meant that they could freeze to death out on the steppes (prairie). Then they had all, including the Russian driver, knelt in the snow beside the sleigh and had prayed earnestly. When they had risen, they saw a little light. They drove there and soon they were in a warm house. Father believed in the answering to prayer.

On October 23, 1910, my sister Anna was born.

In January or February of the year 1912, our Mama became ill. The doctor said she should undergo internal surgery. Father took her to the hospital in Muntau. (See box below.) Every other day he went to see her. Once, probably before the operation, Mama had asked Father if he could bring me along. She wanted to see me once more. The next day Father travelled there again, and I went along. It was very cold. We went in a covered wagon with springs and got there towards evening. Mama, all dressed in white, lay in bed. I sat beside her and she held my hand. I remember that the nurses also brought me supper and I ate beside Mama's bed. The nurses also brought me a picture book. Father had a room for the night at another place, but the nurses wanted me to sleep in a bed in the hallway of the hospital, which I then did. The next day we drove home again.

Father brought our Mama home after some weeks, not that she had recovered fully from surgery, but she was regaining her health. In summer she was well again. Then came the twenty-first of August. Father and a Russian worker were cleaning grain in the storage shed. Mama and the servant girls were doing laundry. Then at noon Mama became ill. She had a miscarriage. Father has written in a book, "I got a midwife immediately." Mama was up and around until evening and then she became very ill. That night we children and grandfather had to sleep in the summer room. After Grandmother's death, Father and Mama with we children had moved into

The new two-story hospital could accommodate 40 patients and had an operating room, x-ray, laboratory, pharmacy, reception area, patient bathing facilities, a large hall for sick children as well as a nurse's residence. The building had hot water heating, warm and cold running water as well as electricity. In 1911 the hospital staff included three doctors, a head nurse, 11 nurses, and a seamstress. This building is now used as a children's sanatorium.[32]

Muntau Hospital, 1912

the little room. I could not sleep. There was light in the whole house, people were walking back and forth. I heard that someone was driving on the yard. Father had gone during the night to get a doctor. He did what he could, but her hour had come. Towards morning, on August 22, Mama died. In the morning before the sun rose, Father came into the summer room. I and my sister Maria got dressed. He took us by the hand and went to the doorway of the little room. There he stopped, we looked in. There lay our Mama on the bed, her eyes shut, she also did not breathe anymore. She was dead. I can imagine how much she must have prayed for me and my siblings in that last night.

Now Mama's body had to be prepared. The funeral was on August 22 (see box below) **at our place in the large shed. I remember Mama lying in the coffin. Father, we children and Grandfather sat near the coffin. Many people had come to the funeral. Of the sermon I do not remember much; I do know that beautiful songs were sung. The coffin was carried to the cemetery. We**

It seems rather unlikely that Dad's mother's funeral occurred on the same day as her death so he may have written "August 22" in error. Many people from the community would have been invited to attend a village funeral which usually occurred a few days after a death.

47

walked behind the coffin. There the coffin was lowered into the grave and the earth was shovelled onto it. We now had no Mama.

Aunt Maria, Mrs. Heidebrecht, took my sister Anna along since she was only a little over a year and a half old. Father hired an older woman as a housekeeper. She made meals, kept the house orderly, and looked after us three children. Anna was at her Aunt Maria's as mentioned previously.

At the beginning of September, I began to go to school. My teacher then was Cornelius Wiens. Once, when the teacher was singing with us, it seemed as if I heard the beautiful songs that were sung at Mama's funeral, and it seemed as if I saw her lying in the coffin. I began to cry. The teacher asked what happened to me. I, however, said nothing. Then the teacher asked if I wanted to go home. At home Father asked what was bothering me. I then told him everything. After a few days the teacher had asked Father, and Father then told him everything. "I noticed it, that this could be what happened to him," the teacher had said.

It was in January 1913 one evening. (It was customary at that time to have the noon meal at twelve, *Faspa* [the evening meal] around four, and supper at nine o'clock. This custom was later discarded. Often, we children were too sleepy to eat supper at that time. We then ate earlier and went to bed.) On this evening in January there were baked potatoes which I like particularly well. I stayed awake in order to eat supper with Father, Grandfather and the others. Father and I sat by the oven and Father said, "Hans, what would you think if I looked for another Mama for you all?" I don't know if I replied, but I was very glad.

Father found another spouse and mother for us children in Barbara Funk from the village of Mariawohl. Yet, before she consented to Father's proposal, she wanted to see the children for whom she would be responsible. Father brought her home to us one day. She took us by the hand and caressed us. She became our mother, and she was a good mother for us children. I will call her Mother here to differentiate from our Mama.

On January 24, 1913, Father and Mother were engaged and their wedding was on February 9th. The wedding was at the home of her parents. As was the custom, the evening before the wedding day was a shower when many gifts were given to the engaged couple. The young people had also recited many poems and presented some skits. Among those who had particularly excelled in reciting poetry was the teacher Johan Wichert who is still living today. He is now over seventy-eight years old. For many years he was elder of the Vineland Mennonite Church. Now he is retired. We children were not at the wedding. (Johann was 45 years old and Barbara was 31 years old at their wedding.)

Johann Neufeld & Barbara Funk Neufeld (1914)
(Is Johann wearing a toupee in this photo?)

Mother was from a more well-to-do family whereas our Mama had been very poor. From her parents, Mother got a full dowry, various pieces of furniture, also a horse and other things. Mother was born on December 16, 1882.

- On November 23, 1913, my sister Agnes was born.
- On November 23, 1915, my brother Gerhard (George) was born.
- On November 21, 1917, my brother Heinrich (Henry) was born.
- On May 31, 1922, my brother Isaac was born.

Father was a complete farmer. He once said, when the plough turned the earth over, he loved the smell of the soil. Now various changes were made. In the large room, linoleum was laid. Shingles were put on the barn and the large storage shed. The machine (Laborgrayka) with which grain had been cut was set aside. Father bought a different rake-machine to cut grain. Instead of sowing summer wheat in spring which did not yield much per acre, Father bought a new variety of winter grain (Bernatky) which yielded much more per acre than the summer wheat. Father was in the process of buying a binder to tie the grain into sheaves. He was also beginning to think of buying a motor to thresh the grain. Sunflower seed or corn was not planted anymore since, he said, it was too hard on the land. He, however, left more land as summer fallow and plowed it well several times. With this process he wanted to retain the moisture in the soil. Thus, Father was inclined to improvements and progress. In our village Father was also one of the most progressive farmers.

War, Revolution, and Famine: 1914 - 1922

Then came August 1914 when World War I began. With the advent of it much came to an end. I recall hearing our neighbour's Russian worker shouting to our worker at the beginning of August when we were bringing in the last load of grain from the field, "Tomorrow we go to war."

At first, we noticed little regarding the war. The young men from our village were conscripted one after the other. As Mennonites, they were not allowed to be at the front with arms, but they had to serve as paramedics (orderlies) in hospitals where wounded soldiers recovered, then also on trains that brought wounded soldiers from the front to Moscow and other cities. The government also took the best of the horses from our village, as also from other villages, but also paid well for them. More and more of the young men were conscripted, including our teacher, Cornelius Wiens. Young teachers with education were now scarce. Finally, an old teacher, Friesen, was hired. He was over sixty years old, did not have the education, also was not able to maintain any discipline in the school either. We did not learn much from him.

I recall Dad telling me of an occasion when Russian officers came to his village to collect as many horses as possible for a war that was still being fought largely with the use of horsepower. As was customary, the officers were fed a generous supper of borscht and bread. After their usual rounds of vodka, Mr. Schmidt who, as an old man still lived near Tofield, brought an officer into the dimly lit barn where he would slap the rumps of several "good" horses while telling the Russians they could take them to the front. Then he pointed to a horse in a dark corner of the barn and said, "that one wouldn't be good for the front." That was because that was a very good horse that was best suited for the spring ploughing without which they would not be able to plant that year's crop. Sometimes it was necessary to bend a statement so that the arc of truth ensured the survival of the family.

Then in the fall of 1915, we heard that the Tsar was contemplating evacuating all German-speaking people and Germans to Siberia. That resulted in much worrying on the part of our parents. Public meetings in the German language were also prohibited at this time. Even in the church, I recall, no sermon was given in German for a short while. The deacons read a message in German then. Nor was there any Christmas program for the children at school.

The fear of deportation came to an end in 1917 when a new government came to power in Moscow. The Tsar had to abdicate. At first there was a provisional government with Kerensky at the head. But this government could not remain in power for long. Then Lenin came to power.

Soon after the Tsar abdicated, the war with Germany also ended. Now the young men from our village, who had been conscripted as paramedics, or who had had to serve in other places, came home one after the other. The teachers who had been conscripted also came home. Our teacher, Friesen, was thoroughly tired of the teaching profession. He was now discharged and in his place two young teachers were hired. They were Abram Nickel and Johan Martens. They both had teacher education and they also had the authority to keep discipline and order. Now we learned in school, much more than we had previously.

Through an agreement with the government in Moscow, the German military occupied Ukraine. That was probably in February of 1917, yet they did not stay long, because a revolution was also starting in Germany in which the emperor of that country also abdicated. The German military withdrew, probably in October or November. Because Ukraine now had no government, many bandits arose. One of the most prominent leaders of these bandits was Nestor Machno. The bandits robbed, plundered, burned, and shot many of the large farmers. Many of our Mennonite farmers, who lived outside the bounds of the Mennonite settlements (villages), were shot. Others fled and came to our villages.

Nestor Makhno, born in 1889 in southern Russia, was imprisoned as an anarchist before World War I but was granted amnesty after the Russian Revolution of 1917. Thereafter, he gathered a militia of mounted terrorists equipped with supply wagons to plunder the Germanic inhabitants consisting of Mennonites, Catholics, and Evangelicals. In many villages, his terrorist army raped the women and executed the men. In the fifteen villages in the settlement of Zagradowka (about 100 kilometres northeast of the present-day city of Kherson which is near the mouth of the Dnieper River), the Makhno band killed 200 people and burned Münsterberg (located in the southwest corner of the Molotschna Colony) and 75 farms between November 29 and December 1, 1919. Already during the First World War, defamatory press articles had incited the general population against

German-speaking Mennonites. Even so, there were isolated incidents of magnanimity from Makhno. He died in Paris in 1934 of tuberculosis at the age of 45. (See box below).[33]

When the German military withdrew in October, some of their soldiers stayed on. They immediately began to organize self-defence units in our villages. Even though the Mennonite ministers spoke out against this, each young man soon walked around with a weapon to protect our villages from the bandits.

My father said that we did not want to have any weapons in the house. He said he was too old, and I was too young, and my brother Peter was younger than I was. Also, my father said the dear God could protect us better than the guns.

Then in January 1918, the bandits (under Machno) joined the Russian army that had come from Moscow. The self-defence units, however, did not want to fight against such a large army. Now it was time to give up their weapons. The bandit leader Machno had, however, said that he wanted to murder all those who were in the self-defence units. That caused great terror. I recall, it was probably February 1st when we were in school, the teacher said we could go home soon after noon. It was a very dark day. When we came home, Father and Mother had already gone to church. There was a prayer meeting. The desire was to pray to the Lord that He might hinder these primitive men from killing everyone. Everyone drove and walked to the church. Never had the church, with a seating capacity of seven hundred, been so full. Never had the people prayed to God so earnestly as on this day. And the loving God answered their prayers.

Nestor Ivanovich Makhno (also known as Bat'ko Makhno) was commander of the Revolutionary Insurgent Army of Ukraine from 1917 to 1921. His supporters attempted to reorganize social and economic life along anarchist lines. These included the establishment of communes on former landed estates, the requisition and egalitarian redistribution of land to peasants, and the organization of free elections to local soviets (councils) and regional congresses. However, the disruption of the civil war precluded a stable territorial base for any long-term social experiments. He is also credited as the inventor of a horse-drawn carriage with a mounted heavy machine gun. [34]

Nestor Makhno: Anarchist and terrorist

On February 2nd everything was still peaceful. I remember that we had no appetite, each person wondered if he would be in eternity the next day. Then came the third of February 1918. The bandits came—a terrible day. People with weapons, guns, were everywhere on the yard, in the house, in every room, in the barn, in the storage shed—everywhere. They looked in every box, took what they wanted, shouted, and swore at times. Mother had to fry eggs and ham and put them on the table. And, without shame as only that type of Russian can be, they ate without forks, just with their fingers. They took clothes, dressed themselves in several pairs of pants, and then put on a set of Sunday best clothes over the others. Some of the soldiers looked very comical. Then they took money, gold rings, and all the watches they could get.

It was during the afternoon when I saw, across the street in Jacob Loewen's yard where many horses and wagons stood, that a young man was running hard and screaming desperately. Then I saw that this young man was shot there among all the wagons and horses. Another young man had been shot at another neighbour's place. Neither of them was from our village. They were from the village of Waldheim and had wanted to hide in our village. Towards evening all these people (we called them Machnowzen) moved on. Father had to go along with them. He came home for the night, however. That was a terrible day. Yet the Lord had heard our prayers—no one from our village had been killed.

Traumatic events like those described above have a way of being mythologized after years of being retold as stories with lessons or "truths" to be passed on to the next generation. After Dad's funeral in 1993, family and relatives were gathered in the common room of the seniors' apartment where my parents lived. Uncle Nick Enns suddenly said, "So you young ones need to hear a story of how God cared for your grandfather during the hard times in Russia." It is unclear whether he then gave an account of the events described above or if it was another occasion when the "Machnowzen" came to Dad's village, ostensibly to terrorise the people and perhaps kill them and destroy the village. Nick, who was five years old at the time, grew up in Pordenau, so it is doubtful that he would have been in Marienthal for the event mentioned above although the people in Pordenau may have had a similar terrifying experience.

In Uncle Nick Enns's telling of the tale, Makhno and his band of terrorists could be seen coming across the steppes from afar, galloping on their horses. He said, "The people in the village ran out into the street, fell on their knees and prayed to God to protect them. And the hand of God came down, and the horses could not penetrate it. They could not penetrate it." He repeated this with emphasis. In my mind this conjured up an image of an enormous hand descending from the sky, men falling off horses rearing up, raging terrorists turning back in fear, just the stuff for a 19th century painter of the Romantic era. I was amazed.

My recollection of one of the rare times Dad spoke to me about "the terrorists" was during the time when Jake Epp was the Minister of Health in the Conservative government of the day. Dad said that, in fear of the "Machnowsen" who were making their way through the villages sowing terror, the people of Marienthal gathered at the church and prayed more fervently than usual before their village meetings. Then Jake Epp's grandfather, a respected member of the village, suggested that some of the men go out to meet Makhno and his gang. So they went and offered the terrorists bread, provisions, and feed for the horses. Knowing that man and beast required nourishment, this elder of the community, who was rather adept at compromise, managed to convince Makno's malitia that the villagers had no weapons, and the terrorists rode away without harming anyone.

I do not know whether the story Dad told me was about the events he wrote (above) or another occasion. His written account would surely have much more veracity than either Uncle Nick's or my recollections as told in stories. However, each version expresses its own moral and ethical "truth" even as the events become mythologized over the decades of telling and hearing that story. Uncle Nick's version of events certainly held our attention as we listened in rapt silence that day.

Nestor Makhno's band of outlaws was the most notable of many militia groups consisting mainly of Ukrainian peasants. However, there were also among them a sprinkling of the disaffected landless Mennonites who felt they had been treated poorly by their co-religionists. The Makhnovites had no overarching ideology to justify their plundering of Mennonite villages, slaughtering some of their victims and often brutally beating the families that were forced to billet them during their time of raiding and anarchy. Historian David Rempel describes the terrorists in his book *A Mennonite Family in Tsarist Russia and the Soviet Union: 1789–1923* in the following quote. His description of the terror in 1918 and 1919 is based on his personal experience as a young man living in the Chortiza region or the "Old Colony," the first Mennonite colony to be established in Russia in the late 18th century.

All combatants, whether Red Army, local bandits, former peasants, or deserters from the tsarist army, forcibly requisitioned anything they wanted. Only the White Army officers occasionally offered to pay, and then only in depreciated tsarist paper money, of *karenki* (small pieces of paper money issued by the provisional government), or equally worthless paper currency issued by a Ukrainian government during the brief months of autonomy given it by the Kerensky regime in the summer and autumn of 1917. Demands by combatants followed a common pattern. Several heavily armed men would burst into a house and with blood-curdling, blasphemous curses, demand money, clothing, food, animals, fodder, bedding, wagons, or whatever else they wanted or thought was available. In the worst cases, and this was especially during the raids in 1919, they killed the head of the household or raped its young women after first forcing them to cook them a meal. These invasions took place at any hour of the day or night. People bold enough to ask an intruder for identification were treated to an assault or at least an explosive string of two-story-high (*dvukh-etazhnye*) or three-story-high (*triokh-etazhnye*) expletives. When the intruders found the doors locked, or if the homeowners did not open them fast enough or demanded a search warrant, they would fire shots through the door or windows and shout, "And here is a permit for you." Should someone have ventured to ask what they were looking for, the answer could have been almost anything: weapons, counter-revolutionaries, food, or simply the opportunity to rummage through the house so that they might find something, anything, that they might consider valuable.[35]

Soon after this, General Denikyn organized an army near the Caucasus Mountains that fought against the Red Army. This newly organized army was usually referred to as the White Army. In the month of June, the White Army had advanced to our village and the Red Army had been beaten back behind the large city of Kharkov. (See box below.) In the next winter the White army under General Denikyn had to retreat and again the Red Army came upon us. Now General Wrangel once more organized an army to fight against the Red Army. But they did not advance much more than to our villages. Several times it happened that our village was held by the White Army in the morning, then in the afternoon by the Red Army, and in the evening the White Army again. Because of so much shooting, no more work was done on the fields. Often, when the shooting was heavy, we sat in the house behind thick brick walls (one foot wide). There were, however, only few deaths during these battles. With time the Red Army gained the upper hand. The White Army retreated, and we were under the Soviet government.

My mother sometimes told us stories of traumatic times in Russia—often enough that I often began to tune them out. Yet, some of those stories do not fade from memory.

Born on March 1, 1916, Mom's birth occurred during the terrible time of the German invasion during World War I. In her telling of that winter (having heard these things from her parents and siblings), the demands of the war left little for the people of the village. Horses were taken for the front. Food was scarce, as was fuel for heating the house. They often had only straw to provide a little heat. Apparently, her mother had a condition where veins in her legs would burst and bleed profusely. Mom often wondered if the rheumatoid arthritis, the cause of so much pain throughout her life, began as a small child due to the difficult pregnancy and birth her mother endured.

During the billeting of soldiers, Mom recounts how Russians from both armies were fed bread and borscht cooked in a large outdoor cauldron

Kharkov (present day Kharkiv) was about 400 kms north of the Molotschna region.

normally used for rendering lard when a hog was butchered. She remembered (or was told by older siblings) how Russian soldiers loved to hold her on their knee because they missed their own children. Mom would have been about three or four years old at the time.

Mom also remembered the trauma of crouching under the window in their house to avoid ricocheting bullets. In another "memory," a Russian soldier entered the house brandishing a knife at her older brother John. Her father took the knife away from the soldier, gave him a loaf of bread, and sent him on his way. Whether this occurred or even whether my recollection of the story is accurate may be doubtful. However, the message to me was that Mennonites did not carry weapons. It was a truth about "bread instead of bullets" that stayed with me.

In 1921 the great famine began in Russia. We also were affected by it. At first, for quite a while, we billeted soldiers for whom we had to provide food. When they retreated, many refugees were sent to us. We also had to submit most of the grain that we still had. We also had no horses anymore to work the land. Father harnessed a cow and a horse which we still had to a plow so that a few acres could be plowed and planted with grain. When the grain had sprouted, Maria, Peter, Anna, and I did the weeding. At this time, we had almost nothing to eat. For breakfast we had *Prips*, that is, roasted wheat or barley used as coffee since we could not get coffee anymore, and we ate a little piece of oatbread, but it was very bitter. For dinner we ate sugar-beet soup. We would eat until we were full, but after an hour we were already hungry again. Many beggars, mostly Russians, stood at the windows and begged. Little could be given to them since we ourselves had almost nothing and there were too many of them. Here and there lay someone that had already died of starvation.

In 1920, several of our ministers, elders, and Mennonite leaders met for a consultation. At this deliberation, a commission was elected that should seek help in Germany, Holland, Canada, and the United States of America for the many starving Mennonites in Russia, and they should also investigate the possibility of emigrating from Russia. In this commission were B. Unruh, A.A. Friesen, and Abe Warkentin. These three men then went to the U.S.A.

and Canada and helped to bring about the American aid that came in 1922. In every village a kitchen was opened in which the American food was cooked. Then the children, the elderly, and the needy could go get it themselves or they could eat it right there. Also, in our family the little children and Grandfather received something from the kitchen. These kitchens helped to prevent more people from dying of starvation.

Johan Rempel, a schoolteacher in the Chortiza Colony, describes the famine in vivid terms as follows.

All rhetoric pales before the grim realities of the famine that ravaged the Ukraine in 1921-1922. I might torture the reader for a long time with staggering facts, facts which seem indeed stranger than fiction. A few examples, however, will be sufficient to show the picture of human suffering as we experienced it in those two years. The causes of the famine were many. First, the area of cultivation had been constantly reduced during the years of the war and civil war, due to the lack of manpower and loss of draft-animals; second, to the depreciation and destruction of agricultural equipment and the inability of the peasant to obtain new ones; third, the drought of 1920 and 1921; last, the voluntary reduction of the sowing area on the part of the peasants themselves, as a protest against the senseless wholesale requisitioning policy of the government. These were, briefly, the causes of the famine.

The catastrophe was made still more horrible by such diseases as cholera and typhus which raged everywhere. We lacked hospital facilities, medicines, trained staff [to combat those and deal with] the indescribable unsanitary conditions in the affected regions. As a result of all this, people died like flies in their homes, on the street, and on the road. Thousands of others left their homes and trekked hundreds of miles into regions where there was still something to eat. Thus, in 1920 thousands of fugitives from the Volga came to the Ukraine, their wagons loaded with household goods, children, women, and the aged, drawn by horses with bones showing through their skins. For months they had been on the road, in rags and filth, living on offal, chaff, bark, and clay, and dying at an appalling rate. And scarcely had they reached the Ukraine when there came the great drought of 1920, but more particularly in 1921. In despair many of them returned to the Volga to die at least in their own homes; for there was no other hope. Others stayed passively awaiting death.

It is now 1921. The famine has reached such a scale that words fail to describe it. The crop was a total failure, the grain mostly being so sparse that it could not be cut with a machine and had to be harvested painstakingly by hand. The people go about emaciated and weak, living as they do mostly on all kinds of refuse. Cases of cannibalism are not wanting, parents and children murdering one another. In a window at the headquarters of the Cheka (Soviet secret police) in a neighboring city almost daily were posted pictures of people who had been condemned to death for cannibalism, in order to deter others from doing the same thing. But hunger knows no fear of punishment. People are digging their own graves for fear that soon they will be too weak to do so and they will remain unburied. But frequently it happens that others bury their dead in graves that someone else had dug for himself or his relations. The dead as a rule are buried naked to save the clothing for the living. And by no means all can afford a wooden box as coffin. One day I saw a place where the father, with four children in the bed, had been dead for two days, the children too weak to leave the bed and call for help. In the same house, but in another room lay two dead Makhnovites, already in a serious state of decomposition. Still in another room of the same building an old laborer, whom I had know very well, probably in a state of delirium, had tried to jump out of the window, but had been too weak and so had died right there, hanging partly out of the window. But why multiply examples. If help does not come soon... I shudder to think of the consequences.[36]

By the time of the famine, Mom was five years old. She often spoke about memories of skeletal figures with extended arms reaching out for food that were indelibly etched in her mind as a child. Mom and her brother, Nick, were sent to the barn where grain had been stored. There they used knitting needles to pick seeds of grain from between the floorboards for extra food. Perhaps it was with memories of the famine that my parents would occasionally say, *"Iss, das du dick und fett wirst"* when he sat down to a table with a generous full meal. "Eat so that you become thick and fat." (Unfortunately, I did just that in my childhood... with no indications of an impending famine.)

With no regard for wealth, ethnicity, politics, or religion, the famine of 1921-1922 spared no one. In many ways, it wreaked a greater carnage on the people of that part of Russia/Ukraine than the civil war had done. The Mennonites may have been spared the worst of the death and destruction because of their agricultural practices, sharing of resources, and because of the aid they received from abroad. The people in the villages of Marienthal and Pordenau where Dad and Mom grew up were located at the farthest eastern corner of the Molotschna Colony. They must have survived the famine with more success than the indigenous peoples of the Ukraine. Unfortunately, famine had followed hard on the heals of a Typhoid epidemic, especially among the Ukrainians and Russians for whom hygiene and sanitation were not priorities. This disease, spread primarily by lice, also spread to Mennonites who were forced to billet military and terrorist militias in their homes.

It was early in the morning of October 31, 1921, that someone came and told Father he was to come to the village office (village soviet). He came back right away and told us he was to prepare himself to go to the village of Waldheim. He took some food along, then he went to the village office and was taken away. Then, in the afternoon we heard that in the village of Waldheim where was the *Wolostamt* (the *Wolostamt* was the office governing several villages) **a commission of three men had come. These men demanded that from each village a certain number of weapons were to be gathered. If the quota of arms was not met, then the men now taken from each village would be shot.**

During the revolution, when the armies went back and forth through the villages, many weapons had been thrown away. Some had gathered these and hidden them. So now, out of each village, two, three or four of the most highly respected men had been taken. From our village Father and Abram

Lepp had been taken. There were quite a few weapons gathered together in our village, too. (See box below.)

I don't quite know the prescribed norm. After several days, Mother, I, and Mrs. Lepp drove to see where Father and Abram Lepp were. We also had to bring them more food. We were told that they were at Richerts' place in the basement. The Richerts had a small factory. Under the factory there was a basement, thirty by thirty feet big. There on the cement floor lay over fifty men who were heavily guarded. The Richerts lived across the street from the factory.

We drove to Richerts and wanted to feed the horses in their barn. They invited us in. Then we noticed that they were very upset. Yesterday six men had been taken from the basement and had been shot behind the barn on the manure pile. We knew some of these men well. We took the food we had brought along to Father and Abram Lepp and spoke with them for a few minutes under strict guard. Father was very calm. He said that nothing more could be done to him than that which was determined for him. Every week we brought him something to eat. After six weeks he was released and came home again.

Grandfather was old. In the last years his memory deteriorated to a great extent. Now he had to be fed and looked after completely. It was 1922 when he lay helpless in bed in the large room. One evening when I was preparing to go to bed, Father came and asked, "Hans, would you keep watch with Grandfather this night? I have not slept for three nights already. I would like to undress again and sleep in bed." Yes, I would sit and keep watch this night. Grandfather lay in bed, the lamp stood on the table, I read the book *Die Familie Pfipferling* (The Family Pfipferling). When I was tired of reading, I sat by the oven and listened to Grandfather as he snored. Then suddenly it seemed as if he stopped breathing, breathed a few more times, I listened,

It has been well-documented that many Mennonites armed themselves in a movement called the *Selbsschutz* (self-protection or self-defence). As a result, many of those villages where guns were prevalent were destroyed. Many Mennonites felt that the *Selbsschutz* was a betrayal of the Anabaptist Mennonite teachings of nonresistance based on Jesus' admonition to "love your enemies, bless those who curse you, do good to those who hate you, and pray for those who mistreat you and persecute you." Matthew 5:44.

and he breathed no more. I took the lamp, went to the bed, and looked. Grandfather was dead. I awoke Father, he was to come to look. When he saw him, he said, "Thanks be to God." Father would gladly have had his father with him yet longer, but he knew this was best for him. Grandfather had often sung the hymn, *Wann schlägt die Stunde, ach wann darf ich gehen Heim, ach nur Heim.* (When strikes the hour, ah, when may I go home, ah only to go home.) The funeral was on February 1st. Because Grandfather had been a minister in the Pordenau Church for many years, the funeral was also in the Pordenau Church. A lot of people also came to the funeral. Grandfather was 89 years and 5 months old when he died.

In the Fall of 1923 Father became ill. He had no pain but was always tired, also coughed more than he usually did, had no appetite, and seemed to lose all interest in anything. When we would ask advice about one thing or another, he would say, "Do whatever you think is best." He mainly lay on a padded seat near the oven. One couldn't get a doctor anymore, and medicine was not to be had. All the home-made remedies that were known were used.

One day in winter on a nice day, Father came to the barn. I was very happy when he came up to the barn. Now things would be better with Father. But he still had no interest in anything anymore. In January 1924, when someone had gone to get a female doctor, she was asked to come to our place. She came, examined Father, said little, also gave no medicine or advice. When she went out, she said to Mother, "Lady, I tell you, your husband has tuberculosis. He will not live more than ten days." Mother told us this and she also told Father. He, however, remained quite calm.

On January 24th I was working in the barn, it was the afternoon, Maria came and said Mother had said I should come in. Mother and we eight children sat in the large room. Father lay on the bench near the oven. He wore the clothes in which he had dressed in the morning. He lay on his side, the one hand under his head. He was still breathing, but his eyes had already gotten dim. We sat there, no one said a word, no one wept. Suddenly Father had breathed his last breath. It seemed as if something mysterious was in the room—as if the angels were carrying his soul to the arms of the Father.

Then suddenly Mother and all the rest of us began to weep. Our father had died. When we stopped crying Mother said, "Go to the neighbours and ask if they will help to prepare our father."

Nickolai Rempel, the minister as well as the director of the choir in our village, had choir practice that evening. He had said, "Let's sing a few songs, then we will go to Mr. Neufeld to sing for him." Then the choir members had said, "He is dead already." He had been quiet for a moment, then with tears he had related that he had visited Mr. Neufeld that forenoon and said how happy he had been at the prospect of soon meeting his Lord.

On the next day, Abram Loewen made the coffin and on January 26th was the funeral. Father was only fifty-five years, four months, and ten days old. He died almost exactly a year after Grandfather was buried. On the day of his funeral, there was a big blizzard so that his brother Gerhard, living only fifteen miles away in the village of Paulsheim, could not come. Only Mother's brother Gerhard and her cousin Heinrich Voth had come. The funeral was in the church. Daniel Janzen and my teacher Johan Martens, who was also a minister, preached at the funeral.

Isaac, my brother, was only one year and eight months old at the time.

We had no horses with which to sow some seed that spring, but loving neighbours came and sowed some acres of land for us. It grew well and we expected to do some harvesting. In the previous year, when Father was still living, my brother Peter once had to go to Uncle Gerhard Neufeld who lived in the village of Paulsheim. My brother Gerhard, who was eight years old, went along. When Peter wanted to come home, Uncle Gerhard had caught a pig of three weeks, put it into a sack, and gave it to Peter. The little pig was not that heavy, but the way home was long. Gerhard, the little boy, had already gotten very tired. Father was very uneasy about Gerhard. He already went often to see if they were coming. The sun began to set. Then Father saw them coming. He went very quickly towards them, took Gerhard into his arms, and carried him home.

This little pig had now become quite a nice hog. Mother said, "Hans, take the pig to Berdjansk, sell it, and then we can buy a horse." Abe Rempel was a peddler who bought all kinds of things—eggs, butter, and much else—these he took to the city and sold them there. He and I hired a driver, we put that big hog at the bottom of the wagon and his eggs and butter at the top. Then we drove to the city of Berdjansk. Towards evening as we drove into the town there stood some Jews on the street. They ran after the wagon and wanted to buy the hog for sixty-five rubles. Abe Rempel, who already was familiar with the Jews, said, "They can't be trusted." In the morning when we came to the marketplace, those same Jews came and wanted to buy the hog but now no one was willing to give more than forty-five rubles. We then drove to the butcher and there sold it for forty-five rubles.

The next day we went home. When we got to our village, we saw that the cattle that usually had been taken to the meadows by this time of day were still in the yards in the village. When I got to our yard, Peter came towards me to tell me that a sickness among the cattle had broken out. Six head of cattle were already dead, and then he told me that our young cow was also already dead. That was a shock. We had put our hopes on that young cow. There she lay dead beside the creek. We would have loved to have taken off the hide to sell but could not since this sickness was very contagious both to people and cattle. Peter and I dug a hole beside her, rolled her in, and buried her.

Late in Fall Mother said, "Hans, go with our neighbour Loewen to the city of Melitopol to buy a horse with the money we have left from the sale of the pig." It was raining and very muddy. In Melitopol, at the marketplace, there were a lot of horses. I bought a white horse which was not very big but looked beautiful for forty-five rubles. Before I drove home, the previous owner sent someone to tell me that the horse was a very stubborn one.

At first, we thought it was a very good horse, but then it showed us that it could be very stubborn. When it didn't want to pull the wagon, then it just would not pull the wagon. We could beg it with kindness, then get angry and whip it very hard, but it would not pull the wagon. It only pulled the wagon when it felt like it. Soon we bought another good horse so that we had two good horses and this bad one. Now things went a little better from a material perspective. We could plant and harvest. The government also did not take everything away. It was possible to buy and sell more.

Since I had to do so much thinking as to how to progress materially, I did not participate in all the social activities of the young people but rather participated in prayer and Bible study on Sunday evenings. I was more interested in that. My sister Maria also did not join in all the social life. We were often at home on Sunday afternoons.

I knew that Jesus had also come for me; I loved my Lord, and in the Spring of 1925, I partook in the catechism instructions. That was something very wonderful, very valuable for me. At Pentecost, on June 2, 1925, I was baptized by Elder Aron Regehr and became a member of the Pordenau Mennonite Congregation. Why I became a member of the Pordenau Mennonite Church instead of the Rudnerweide Congregation where Father and Mother were members I will write about later.

Preparations for Emigration

I have already written that when the difficult years began in Russia, our Mennonite leaders sent a delegation of three men to Canada and the United States to solicit help for the starving Mennonites in Russia. As a result of its efforts, MCC sent relief to Russia. These men also worked for the possibility for the Mennonites in Russia to emigrate to Canada.

At this time in Canada, a Board of Immigration and Colonization was organized in Rosthern, Saskatchewan, whose chairman was Elder David Toews. Through his efforts, 20,000 Mennonites were able to emigrate to Canada in the next few years. Also, at this time, the *Menno Verband* (Menno Association) was begun whose chairman was B. B. Janz. This board worked towards improving our economic lot under the Soviet government but also dealt with emigration to Canada. Through this board we got our visas to go to Canada. Already in 1923, a group from the Old Colony left for Canada. Then, in 1924 a group of over a thousand people left from the Lichtenauer Station on the Molotschna River. Again in 1925, a large group left from the Stulnewo Station, also over 1000 souls. (See top box on p 68.) Most of these got credit from the CPR (Canadian Pacific Railway) to make their trip. (See middle box on p 68.)

Once, when Mother's siblings were together in 1925 in Mariawohl, they had talked about emigrating. They also all wanted to emigrate. Then, one of her brothers had said, "Then we have to see to it that our sister, Mrs. Johann Neufeld, also comes along." Mother's brother-in-law, Heinrich Wichert, had taken on the responsibility of getting the necessary documents. When Mother was informed of their plans, she was immediately willing to go. I, however, was not very interested in this proposal. But God had other plans for me and for our family. He did not want us to go through the great affliction that was to come on our people in the 1930s. Through the Lord God's guidance, all of us, our whole family, was able to emigrate. (See bottom box below.)

First, I had to get documents from the village Soviet which Mr. Wichert then took to the Menno Association in order to get the visas. Then Mr. Wichert and a representative from each family had to go to the city of Melitopol to have another government official sign other documents. Mr. Wichert was working (obtaining documents) for five or six families. We travelled there by train. That was my first ride on a train. I had some peculiar experiences on this trip of which I may write later. Mr. Wichert then travelled to Karkow with our documents from where we were to receive our

---

Stulnewo may be present-day Stul'neve near Tokmak on the northern periphery of the Molotschna Mennonite Settlement.

In 1925 the *Railway Agreement* was signed by the Canadian Pacific and Canadian National Railways and the Canadian government providing for the railways to recruit immigrants including those from the "non-preferred" countries of northern and central Europe. More than 185,000 central Europeans entered Canada under the agreement (1925-1929).[37]

"The great affliction" was probably a reference to the Holodomor (death by hunger) inflicted on the Ukrainian population during the famine of 1931-1932. Attributed to collectivisation and the oppressive means by which the Stalinist regime subjugated the population of Ukraine, an estimated 3.5 to 5 million people died of starvation. Many Mennonites from the Molotschna region were deported to Siberia. The prosperous villages of Marienthal and Pordenau no longer exist.

Train loading immigrants in Lichtenau, Molotschna (1924)

passports. Our family needed five passports. Mother, I, Maria, Peter and Anna, each needed one. The others, Agnes, Gerhard, Heinrich and Isaac, were on Mother's passport. At first very little had to be paid for passports, but when we wanted to get ours, we had to pay double the amount of the earlier passports. Mr. Wichert also had to travel to Karkow several times before he got them.

At that time the Canadian Government had a doctor in Russia who would examine the emigrants and, if he found them to be healthy, they would be allowed to emigrate to Canada. On May 26, 1926, a Canadian doctor, Dr. Drury, came to our settlement. We had to come to the village of Alexandertal where Dr. Drury would examine our family. He declared everyone healthy except my brother Gerhard. He had a spot on his head, approximately two inches in diameter, where the hair had come off and he had a scabies rash. Gerhard was ten years old at that time. But Mr. Wichert said, by the time we would get to Moscow where Dr. Drury would have to inspect us once more, the spot would have healed. (See box below.)

Once before, Mother and I had been at Mariawohl together with her relatives. There they spoke of emigrating. At that time, I was asked to estimate the amount of money we would get if we sold our farm (*Wirtschaft*) and all that we had. I said I thought we could sell our farm for 500 rubles. Then we also had grain that would bring in another 500 rubles and for our furniture and implements we should get another 500 rubles. All together that would be 1500 rubles, but that would only be half of what we would need for our ship fare. We needed about 3000 rubles. Where should we get the rest of the money? The C.P.R. was not willing to provide credit anymore. Mr. Wichert, however, knew what to do. The Russian government allowed

In *Hard Passage* Arthur Kroeger writes that receiving permission to emigrate involved documentation from a variety of officials in cities often located some distance from where a Mennonite family lived. These documents required clearance for any tax liabilities from the finance department, any outstanding military obligations from military authorities, and clearance from the police and the chairman of the regional soviet. Dr. Drury's examination was a particularly difficult hurdle for the Neufeld family to overcome because families could be denied emigration based on a medical condition of any member of the family.[38]

only so much money, a certain sum, to be taken with each passport. He said there would be those who had more money than they could take out. They would lend us the money and, when we were in Canada and were earning, we could repay them. (See box below.)

We gave notice that on a particular day we would sell our farm by open auction. On that day only five or six people who wanted to buy the farm had come. When they were through, the last bid was not 500 rubles but 1901 rubles. We then sold the grain for 500 rubles and, a few days before we left, we had an auction of furniture, implements and all that we had to which many Russian people from surrounding Russian villages came. From this auction sale we also got 1500 rubles. We now had enough money for the ship fare and to pay for all that was necessary. The good Lord knew exactly how much we needed.

June 15, 1926 was the day determined for our departure. On the previous evening, the neighbours wanted to have a farewell party (*Abschiedsfest*). Our large machine shed was empty. The neighbours brought benches and, before we knew it, the large machine shed was filled. They came—old and young and also children, rich and poor, big and small. The minister, Aron Braul, and the teacher, Johan Marten, had farewell sermons. Afterwards, most of the people came and shook hands with us. Once more— the last night—we slept in our house. God the Lord held his protective hand over us. We did not think even once that someone would come to rob us.

The CPR had provided many Mennonites left destitute by the revolution and years of drought and famine with a loan known as *Reiseschuld*, travel debt. Immigrants began repayment immediately when the crops in Canada were good. However, during the depression of the 1930s it became increasingly difficult for farmers to make payments. After 1930 the CPR ceased to charge interest on the loans in an attempt to ease the financial burden for distressed farmers. It was only in 1946 that the Canadian Mennonite Board of Colonization was able to retire the debt largely due to the tenacity of David Toews. Final payments of the debt of over 2 million dollars were made to the CPR in November of 1946. Three months later, Toews died, his work having provided a new life in Canada for over 2000 Mennonites.[39] Fortunately, the Neufeld family was able to pay for its transportation through the proceeds of the sale of their farm and thus avoided the hardship of travel debt during the first years in Alberta.

Neufeld Family with Neighbours. June 1926

((Left to right) Neighbour with child, Anna, Barbara, Isaac, Maria, Neighbour & child, John, Neighbour, Agnes, Henry, Peter, George, Neighbour

Only one month later, Father's brother, our Uncle Gerhard Neufeld, was shot on the night after their auction sale. I have written about that already.

Then on June 15, at 3:00 o'clock in the afternoon, the neighbours came, loaded us and our things on their horses and took us to the station in Nelgowka. As we rode along the street of our village, people stood outside all over and waved goodbye. As long as I could, I looked back at our village. Never would I see it again. I had lived in it for twenty-one years.

In 1927 Stalin's campaign against the kulaks, farmers with modest land holdings and a few cattle, resulted in about 850,000 people being deported to Siberia. Among them were many Mennonites. That same year only 847 Mennonites were allowed to emigrate, among them the parents of renowned operatic tenor, Ben Heppner, who settled in the Dawson Creek area. In 1928 only 511 were allowed to leave. In 1929 some Mennonites managed to obtain passports and exit permits from the administration of the Soviet Union, known for its inconsistency. As a result, about 10,000 Mennonites sold their property in the colonies and went to Moscow seeking exit permits. The Soviet government was ready to allow them to emigrate to Canada and the CPR was prepared to provide loans for resettlement, but the Canadian government refused to accept them because of rising unemployment in Canada.

> Prime Minister King remained well disposed towards the Mennonites, but the deterioration of the economy generated rising public resistance to immigration. In 1929, the Toronto Labour Council declared itself "absolutely opposed" to the admission of the Mennonite refugees. Groups such as the Orange Lodge regarded immigration from Europe as a Catholic and French-Canadian plot against Canada's British institutions.[40]

Under the Canadian constitution immigration was a shared responsibility of both provincial and federal governments. With an impending election the following year, King deferred to prairie provincial governments that were against further immigration.

In 1930, with the new Conservative government under Prime Minister R. B. Bennett, immigration came to an end. Approximately 8000 Mennonite refugees were stranded in Moscow. While friends and relatives still managed to bring 1123 of them to Canada, most were deported to Siberia in January and February. Traveling in unheated boxcars, many froze to death. Others died of exposure to the extreme cold when they were left in the desolate Siberian countryside. Among those fortunate enough to arrive in Canada were the future parents of Alberta novelist Rudy Wiebe whose novels paint a picture of the Mennonite experience in Canada.

During the depression of the 1930s, the Canadian government refused to extend relief (welfare) to non-citizens. They included impoverished immigrants who came from any country not part of the British Empire, some of whom were deported back to their countries of origin because of their poverty. It was due to the efforts of David Toews and B.B. Janz that no Mennonites were deported from Canada back to the Soviet Union. Through the Canadian Mennonite Board of Colonization, they sent assistance to needy Mennonite families in the form of food, clothing, and medical care whenever possible, despite limited financial resources.[41]

In reading Dad's memoir, it is interesting to note that his family managed to survive the depression with farm produce and the goodwill of a non-Mennonite neighbour. When they could no longer make payments on the farm purchased from Mr. Lingrell, Dad offered to return it to him. Mr. Lingrell simply requested that they pay the taxes on the land so that the government couldn't repossess it, as happened to many farmers in Alberta who were unable to pay the yearly taxes levied on their property during the depression.

Journey to Canada

When we were at the station at Nelgowka, the others, for whose departure Mr. Wichert had worked, came; H. Wicherts, Mrs. Fransen with her large family, Jacob Kutz and Abe Barg. Only the Heinrich Funks (Mother's brother) were not yet ready. Our things—we had four large boxes—were put on the train and we all boarded, and at 10:00 in the evening we left on the train. The following morning, we were at the large city of Kharkov. Towards evening we came to the city of Orol. Before dark we went through the city of Tula, and the following morning, June 18, we came to Moscow. (See box below.)

Barbara (Funk) Neufeld's diary

Excerpts from Barbara (Funk) Neufeld's diary have been inserted into Dad's memoir to give a fuller picture of the experience of emigration and a new beginning in Canada for the Neufeld family. Barbara's experience of those years was filled with heart-breaking difficulties and fraught with unimaginable challenges for a woman who was responsible for eight children. During this time, the eldest children—Dad at 21 years of age, Maria at 19, Peter at 17, and Anna at 15—all took on adult responsibilities that saw the family safely arrive first in Saskatchewan and then in northern Alberta the next year. Barbara had another child, Greta, of whom we know very little. She was already married with a family in 1926 at the time of her mother's emigration to Canada.

Edgar Rogalski writes in *Diary of Johann Neufeld and Barbara Funk Neufeld: From the Russian Revolution to Pioneer Life in Peace River, Alberta,*

Greta (Margareta) Funk was the daughter of Barbara Funk, born out of wedlock in 1900. No one knows the circumstances of her father's heritage or how Barbara came to have a child when she was eighteen. Secrecy and silence surrounded the life of Greta in the Neufeld family. Greta, along with her husband and three children managed to escape from the Soviet Union in 1929. They arrived in San Francisco along with other Mennonite refugees. She lived in Dinuba, California, and visited her mother several times in Tofield, Alberta.

Dad's stepmother noted in her diary that they arrived on June 17 rather than June 18. Her account may be more accurate because Tula is only about 180 kilometres from Moscow suggesting that they would have arrived on June 17.

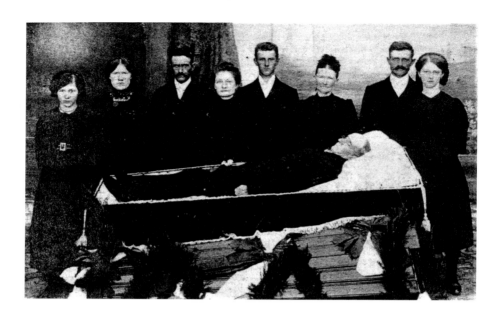

Barbara (Funk) Neufeld's family in Mariawohl
(L to R) Elizabeth (Funk) Wichert, Aganetha Funk Dick, Johann Neufeld, Barbara Funk
Neufeld, Gerhard Funk, Aganetha Foth Funk, Heinrich Gerhard Funk, Greta Funk
(Barbara's daughter), Gerhard Funk (deceased in coffin)

Tuesday, June 15, 1926 *(See box below.)* We left Marienthal at 3:00 pm and then at 10:00 pm we left Pologe. On the 17th of June we arrived in Moscow at 9:00 in the morning. It was 6:00 pm when we arrived at our lodgings. Gerhard had to go immediately to the Commission and did not get through. Tuesday we will go again to the doctor.

The Mariawohler [Fransen and Funk families] *left* [Moscow] *on June 19th at 11:00am and hope to go across the border on the 20th of June. When I heard the news that Gerhard could not come along, I lost all hope. My emotions were beyond what anyone could possibly imagine.*

The date is written as June 15th. However, the dates referred to under June 15th include those days up to June 19th. Therefore, Barbara must have intended to write June 19 or 20 at the time of writing.

My relatives were happy and prepared to further their journey and I just have to wonder what is going to happen to us. They all gathered at the railway station, and then they left by train and we are left behind. I must stay here with the family. I wanted to send half of my family but that is not possible. It is very expensive here and every day we have to walk up 58 steps to our otherwise quiet and adequate lodgings.

We all took lodging at the Ukrainsky Gostinieza (Ukrainsky Gasthaus Hotel). On the following day, Uncle Wichert and I went with Gerhard (George) to the Russcapa (Russian Canadian Pacific Railway and Steamship Company). We first wanted to see the Canadian doctor, Dr. Drury, regarding George so that he could get the documentation to emigrate to Canada. Dr. Drury was, however, on a trip and would return after a week. We were to wait. The others—Heinrich Wicherts, Mrs. Fransen and her family and others—left Moscow the following day on June 19th. We, however, could not go.

I went almost every day to the Russcapa to see if Dr. Drury was back. One day I was told I should take George to a well-known doctor, also a professor. If he declared George healthy, we could continue our travel. On the following day, I took George with me and searched for this doctor's office. The doctor, I've forgotten his name, examined the spot on George's head for a long time, then he gave me a letter and said I was to take George on the following day to a chemical laboratory where they would thoroughly examine him. On the following morning George and I went again and found the building. It was a large house but dilapidated. On the lower floor all the windows were broken. This could not be the laboratory. Yet the house number was correct. We went up the steps to the second floor where we saw that we were at the right location. There was a man to whom we gave the letter from the doctor-professor. He examined the place on George's head, took a sample of the scabies, examined it through his microscope, and then gave us a letter to give to the doctor-professor.

When I got out onto the street, I looked at the letter. There I saw among other words the word "na naydeno" (nothing found) of bacilli that were contagious.

When we returned at noon and showed the letter to Mother and the other siblings, we were all very happy. The Lord had held that man's eyes, since we knew this was something contagious because Henry and Isaac had already caught it. That afternoon I again took George to the doctor-professor. When he saw the letter, he declared George healthy and gave us a letter for the Russcapa. On the following morning I took the letter to the Russcapa. When they saw this letter, they began to work quickly with our papers, and the next evening, July 3, we were to depart from Moscow. We hired a driver to take our baggage to the station. We ourselves took a streetcar.

When we were in the station, I suddenly saw the little Jew from the Russcapa who took the immigrants onto the train. Suddenly he called all the immigrants into another room and then took them all into the train. There were Russians, Jews, Germans, but only a few of our Mennonites. Around midnight, the train departed.

We had been in Moscow for fifteen days. For the hotel we had to pay quite a lot. Mother wrote in her diary that each day we had to go up fifty-eight steps. (Mother had terrific headaches from time to time. Now in Moscow, when she had so much to worry about, they were even more intense. Then my sister Mary had to concern herself with meals and other things.)

I must say, I have only seen a little of Moscow, since I always had to go with George. Today, when I think back, I don't know how I found all the addresses where we had to go since I had never been in a large city and only seldom in a small city. My brother Peter was not kept so busy and was able to see more of Moscow.

The following afternoon, we came to the border post, Sebesch [at the border between Russia and Latvia]. Here we all had to disembark. Our passports were inspected as were all our boxes and suitcases. When we were all back on the train, it went slowly through the Red Gate. We looked out of the window and saw the Red Gate. Now we were out of Russia. The train stopped and the Latvian conductors embarked. We were now in Latvia.

The following day, July 5, we came to Riga. Here in Riga, all immigrants had to undergo a thorough cleaning. We had to wash, bathe, and there was also a vapour bath (steam bath). Our clothes were all disinfected, all insects—lice, etc—were exterminated. Here also the hair of the women and girls were combed thoroughly. Many had their hair cut short. My sisters also allowed their hair to be cut instead of having them combed for hours.

On the following day, we again had to appear before the doctor. We feared that he would not let us travel on because the three boys, George, Henry and Isaac, still had the sore spots on their heads. Someone had already told us, the doctor is a Jew, he very much loves money. When our family came before him, he said, no, he could not let us travel on. Mother and I pleaded earnestly that he should let us travel. I finally said I would give him some money. Then he said, "Be quiet or I will let you be imprisoned." To sit in prison was the last thing I wanted to do in Riga. But he immediately gave me his address and said he would be home after 5:00 pm. I searched for the street and the house. He was already at home. I put $10.00 on the table, he wrote his signature on the papers, and we were ready to travel on.

The following day, July 9, we embarked on a ship and sailed away. Mother wrote in her diary, the voyage on this little ship went quite well. It was very beautiful when we went through the Wilhelms Canal. (See box below.) I have forgotten what the name of the ship was.

Thursday, July 8, 1926 ...we think we are leaving on the 9th in the morning. We had to wait for about three hours. There was a lot of things to see, big buildings, lots of greenery, lots of lights, all kinds of ships, big ones and little ones, big bridges through which we had to pass and the gate (lift bridge) *that was opened for a ship and was also opened for us. We are now in Germany and everything is built up on both sides of us. It didn't get dark until 10:30 at night, we were tired and went to sleep, otherwise we would have seen more during the night.*

Here we are still being examined and watched. So far, we have been spared, but who knows what will become of us. Oh, if only the children were not so restless, then I would be able to enjoy this more. It is because of the

---

The Kaiser Wilhelm Kanal, now known as the Nord-Ostsee-Kanal (North Sea to Baltic Sea Canal), runs 98 kms from Brunsbüttel to Kiel in the German state of Schleswig-Holstein.

children that I have so many headaches, yet I have One whom I can trust. He has promised to be Father to widows and orphans. He will also be our advisor because He has guided and protected till now. We cannot thank Him enough. To Him be praise, honour and thanksgiving for all that He has done for us. (See first box below.)

On July 13 we arrived in London. Here we had to embark on the train that was to take us to Southampton. In Southampton there was a large building that had been built for American soldiers during World War I.

Now the CPR. and the CNR (the Cunard and Pacific ship companies) had rented this for the immigrants. This was the last place where immigrants going to Canada had to come before the doctor. Here many were kept back because of illness; they were healed and then they could travel further. (See second box below.)

On the following day, we also came before the doctor. We—I, Mary, Peter, Annie, and Agnes—each got a white card that meant that we could go on. Mother, however, and the three boys got blue cards. Mother and the boys, George, Henry, and Isaac, were immediately put into another building under quarantine. Mother wasn't even permitted to separate our clothing from their clothing. Now my sister Mary had to take Mother's role. She had to put Mother's and the boys' clothing in one suitcase and bring it to her.

We were then taken to the train the evening of July 15. Through the night we travelled across England to Liverpool where we embarked on the large ship Montcalm on July 16. I don't know anymore how many days we were

---

Barbara sometimes ends her diary entry with prayer-like sentences voicing her thanksgiving and trust in God.

In 1922 the Atlantic Park Hostel Co. Ltd. was established ten miles north of Southampton, England, by a consortium of the shipping companies, Cunard, White Star, and Canadian Pacific. The vacant American aircraft hangars were converted into dormitories, dining rooms, kitchens, bathrooms, medical facilities, etc., designed to bring immigrants together in one place where they could be provided with food, lodging and medical care. Here immigrants were protected from unscrupulous people in the City of London who would take advantage of them while they waited for passage to Canada and the U.S.[43]

on this large ship. [I have noted, seven days.] (See box below.) **Many became seasick. I was somewhat seasick for two days. My sister Mary, however, was not seasick at all. She helped here and there when a mother was very sick and could not look after her children.**

Atlantic Park Hostel. Converted airplane hangars used to house trans-migrants in Southhampton.[44]

Dad added this note to his memoir at a later date.

Immigrants at Atlantic Park in 1926. Barbara is seated in the second row with the women, sixth from the right, behind the girl with the white collar. The three boys in the front row slightly to her left appear to be George, Isaac, and Henry.[45]

Neufeld family in Southampton, waiting for transit to Canada.
Gerhard (George), Agnes, Anna, Barbara, Isaac (on Barbara's lap), Maria, Heinrich, Hans (Johann), Peter. (Perhaps the short hair was the result of the "thorough cleansing" in Riga.)

PIER 21 SHIPS

MONTCALM (III)

Ship Name History: Montcalm (III) - HMS Wolfe

Builder: John Brown & Co Ltd, Glasgow

Length: 550 ft.

Width: 70 ft.

Gross Tonnage: 16418

Funnels: 2

Masts: 2

Engines: Steam turbines (double-reduction)

Capacity: 542-cabin, 1268-3rd class passengers

Speed: 16

Completed: December, 1921

Out of Service: November 7, 1952

Canadian Pacific - armed merchant cruiser

Immigrant ship, Montcalm

Here begins Barbara Neufeld's account of the time spent in England with the three boys, Gerhard, Heinrich and Isaac, while they were recovering from scabies. (See first box below.)

Tuesday, July 13, 1926. On Tuesday we arrived in London around 5:00 o'clock. A couple of hours after everything was in order (emigration papers?) *we boarded a train. We had travelled quite a long distance and arrived in England* (Southampton?) *around 11:00 o'clock* (in the evening?). *We saw lush green countryside, many streets and a lot of big buildings, even more than those in Riga. There were also a lot of big trees and big stores beyond anything I could have ever imagined.*

When we arrived in London (Atlantic Park Hostel in Southhampton?), that was Tuesday night, the 13th of July, we were brought into a big hall and given tea and white bread. We slept in this hall, and in the morning, we washed and combed our hair. We were bathed and examined by a doctor which was not as bad as I had imagined it to be. The next day, however, we were called individually to see the doctor. The doctor gave me a blue card and told me to go see the nurse who took me and the three little ones to a house. The other five children had to wait for us while we were directed to a room and told to wait until the doctor came to talk with us. So, I sat and waited. It felt as though the door behind us was locked. Who knows how long we will have to wait to get out of this building until we are allowed to go out? (See second box below.)

Scabies (Sarcoptes scabiei) is caused by a mite that burrows into the skin and causes severe itching. Scabies can be highly transmissible between people who are in close contact, often in unsanitary conditions. Henry and Isaac likely contracted scabies from George on the land journey from Marienthal to England. Recovery time, once considered to be four weeks and longer, included treatment with an insecticidal ointment administered to the whole body for at least eight to fourteen hours to kill the mites and their eggs before washing it off the body.

Operating under the 1922 Aliens Order which required that all aliens entering Britain be medically inspected, it allowed immigration officers to refuse entry to those with medical conditions.[46]

They told us how things were going and that they had taken the five other children away and that they would soon bring us something to eat. We then learned what was going to happen. The five children (Hans, Mariechen, Peter, Anna, and Agnes) left on Thursday the 15th of July at 11 o'clock at night. They have the privilege of getting the best places. I don't know if that is true or not. I was not even allowed to help with the packing but had to sit under lock and key. I have been sitting here for four days already.

Today is Monday morning (July 19). Who knows what the day will bring? I really don't know. The first day I cried and then I spent the second day crying. On the third day they (other Mennonites) came and sang for me and I felt comforted. I received visitors every day and this too helped to cheer me up.

They have rinsed out Heinrich's eyes and smeared some salve on them. Now they want to see how things will look tomorrow. They only came on Monday to examine him, that is, after five days. On the 20th of July the nurse came and cleaned Heinrich's eyes and bandaged them again. They haven't even looked at the others (Gerhard and Isaac).

Wednesday, July 21st in the morning. The weather is cold all day. They have bathed Heinrich's eyes again and smeared salve on them. Today we had to go to the doctor. When we were there, the doctor said that we must wait until we are finished and there are only a few more (patients). After they were all finished it was our turn. He then said that he did not have time and we should wait until tomorrow. That is the way it often happens to us. It is so depressing here. When you get in here and live here it is really bad, but how does one get out of here? The situation is so depressing for me.

Friday, July 23rd. We have already seen the nurse. She has put new bandages on me but has not put salve on my eyes. I have a very hard life with my children. I have a lot of headaches.

On July 23, we arrived in Quebec City. We were immediately taken to the train that should take us across Canada to Rosthern. In Montreal, a Mr. Wieler boarded the train. He was from the Mennonite Board in Rosthern and came to meet the Mennonite immigrants. He gave us *Der Bote* and *Die Mennonitische Rundschau* to read. (See box on p 86.) He also helped us to proceed wherever he could.

(See Appendix 3, page 186, for immigration documents titled *Canadian Government Return, Canadian Immigration Service* found in the archives of the *Canadian Museum of Immigration at Pier 21* in Halifax. *Part 1* of the form documents the first arrival of members of the Neufeld family. *Part 2* lists the arrival of Barbara with George, Henry, and Isaac. *Part 3* is a listing by the *Canadian Mennonite Board of Colonization* of the first group of Neufeld children to arrive and *Part 4* lists the arrival of Barbara and the three boys. Parts 5 and 6 show the arrivals of the Enns family in Canada.)

Saturday, July 24th. *My neighbour has been allowed to leave the quarantine quarters and I am now alone. It is better to be alone than in the quarantine with someone else. I don't know how long we will have to stay here. We were at the doctor's again today and I received a thorough examination, but they did not bother with Heinrich, Gerhard and Isaac.*

Monday, July 26th. *We have been bandaged again for what was not done right yesterday. I have already written two letters today, one to Marienthal and the other to Greta. We had a wonderful meal today, fried fish, butter, jam, milk, and white bread as well as tea with lemon. For lunch we had a delicious soup with potatoes, gravy, and roasted lamb with Kompott, that is cooked fruit, white bread, and tea. For supper we had fish, tea, white bread, butter, jam, and milk.*

In Moscow we had bought tickets to Colonsay, Saskatchewan, where Mother's uncle Peter Voth lived. Since Mother had stayed in England, and we did not know her uncle, we had taken tickets to Rosthern. When the train stopped at Colonsay for a few minutes, we saw Uncle Peter Voth at the station. We talked with him. He asked, "Why are you not staying here? There is now a lot of work here."

We got to Rosthern on July 27. In Rosthern there was an immigrants' house to which we were taken. Daniel Enns of the Board bought us some flour, sugar, coffee, and other foodstuffs. Mary, my sister, now made us the first meal since we had left Russia. On the ship we had always received meals and on the train we mainly just ate lunches. The next day a farmer came already to take Mary to work for him, so we had no cook anymore.

Peter travelled to Colonsay the next day to see if anyone would take us in. He phoned immediately that Mother's uncle Peter Voth and Gerhard Berg (Mrs. Berg was the Voths' daughter) would take us in. We packed everything and on July 30th travelled with all our goods to Colonsay, Saskatchewan.

Friday, July 30th. Today we feel homesick. We really miss our loved ones. Have had our shirts and clothes washed today. This helps to pass the time of day. Today they brought us three handkerchiefs (6 pence), two cans for chalk (3 pence), one pencil for one pence and a brush for 6 pence. A bar of soap for 3 pence, two pounds of apples for 8 pence, for a total cost of 27 pence.

Sunday, August 1st. I received a lot of visitors today but my children are so unruly, so much so that I count the minutes until I can have some peace and quiet. Sometimes I am at my wit's end. Sometimes it is just better to be alone than to have visitors. I have had headaches for two days in a row. I have a really difficult life here.

Monday, August 2nd. Today my tears won't stop coming. I cried a lot. To my way of thinking, they have forgotten me. On Saturday they changed the bandages for the first time. Sunday, I did it myself, and today it was suppertime before they came. They come and examine us and let us sit from one day to the next and the time is going so slowly that I just cannot describe how slow it is. My room is very small and very hot. It is very hot inside and the flies buzz around my head and there is no way to darken the room.

Friday, August 6th. Yesterday we saw Dr. Hummel and he promised us that we would be able to leave on Saturday, but who knows which Saturday that will be. Now we are hopeful that it will happen. Up until now we had given up all hope. We will probably be told that all the hair must grow over the bald spots before we can leave. It is raining again today. We have had our dressings changed but now we only get them changed once per day.

Monday, August 9th. I dream every night about my husband and about my parents, the dreams are so vivid. Now I also dream about my relatives, Heinrich Funks, that they are already in England, and I also dream that the news about

Gerhard Neufeld is not as bad as they say it is. When I wake up, I am homesick and in tears.

We have had our dressings changed again. Dr. Hummel called our name, but we were not told that he called for us. I don't know if it is good or bad that we did not have an appointment. Next Saturday, August 21st, is the date that Dr. Hummel promised us that we could leave. We wait with renewed optimism for that day to come.

Sunday, August 15th, a really nice day and a good morning. Things went quite well. After Faspa (supper) I had a lot of visitors. Men and women sang for me and prayed with me. We had a blessed time together. May God hear all the prayers that we have lifted up to Him, that we may reach our goal. May the Lord give us patience so that we can persevere and that we will eventually all meet together in heaven. Then there will be no more goodbyes. We will be forever with the Lord in eternity.

Thursday, August 19th, a pleasant morning. Until now we assume that we will be leaving this Saturday. The doctor and the agent have both said that we can leave, but today we were suddenly told that the ship is full, and they begin to hint at bribes. I feel so heavy and I begin to worry about what is to become of us.

Monday, August 23rd. It is dark, cool, and sad. It seems to me that there is no way out of this and sometimes I almost despair, also because of the children. I sometimes think that there is no mercy for me.

Wednesday morning, August 25th, a beautiful day. Today the following families arrived: Jacob Thiessens, Jacob Loewens, Jacob Ennses, Papkins (Paetkaus?). (See box below.)

Friday, August 27th. Cold in the morning but a really nice day because of the children. There are 17 children to chase each other around, two babies and 10 children in the hospital and 10 women. The Marienthaler (people from her family's village in Molotschna) visited me. That really made me happy. May God grant them a safe journey and for us a happy reunion (with family).

> The Ennses would have been Mom's family.

Wednesday, September 1st. It rained during the night, it is still raining. We are experiencing very difficult circumstances here. Today we are permitted to leave the quarantine. We were in the great hall for 7 weeks. How long will we still have to stay here? I just don't know. May God allow us to leave soon to join my children. I am truly thankful that our beloved Saviour has been gracious to me until now and that our health has been restored.

Barbara Neufeld continues to write about her difficulty with poor health due to the persistent headaches and her feelings of abandonment. On Sundays there was often a church service, Sunday School for the children, and then a prayer service. These services, held with other Mennonites who were being processed for immigration on their way to Canada, would have been in German. Barbara and the children were destined to remain in England until the middle of October.

Wednesday, September 29th. Today Tante Neufeld (Mrs. Neufeld, Gerhard Neufeld's wife, Maria) *arrived with Onkel Friesen* (see box below) (Mr. Friesen, Maria's father) *and many others from the village of Heirschau* (Molotschna). *Oh, what happened in Paulsheim is so terrible! We can be so thankful that we were already here. I never want to go back there. Onkel Gerhard Neufeld* (Barbara's brother-in-law and Dad's uncle) *was shot on July 16th. He lived for 14 hours and then he was a corpse. How terrible! He died in Halbstadt and then he was brought home and was buried on the 20th of July 1926. And in Hierschau they shot Peter Dueck on the 23rd. He died immediately. Then on an August night in 1926 three men and one woman were severely wounded and Neufeld's Wilhelm was also severely wounded and almost beaten to death.* (Willy Neufeld, 1907 – 1997, is Gerhard's son who was beaten when his father was shot.) *Our Heinrich was taken to the hospital on the 27th of September.*

Monday, October 4th. They discharged him (Heinrich) *today and let him come home.*

Tante and *Onkel* were Mennonite terms used to address adults for "Mrs." and "Mr." instead of the German *Frau* and *Herr*. *Tante* and *Onkel* also translate as aunt and uncle in High German as in, for example, *meine Tante und mein Onkel* (my aunt and my uncle).

Wednesday, October 13th. *Yesterday we saw Dr. Megi and he said that we can leave without conditions. Now we are waiting for Dr. Hummel and, if he says "healthy" and if it is God's will, then maybe we can leave.*

Oh, how happy we will be when we can finally leave. Then I think I will cry for joy. I received a letter from Maria on the 10th of October and one from Hans on the 12th and also one from Agnes on the same day. I sent them a letter on the same day. On the 2nd of October, the children of G (Gerhard) Neufeld left (for Canada). *I have tried to understand why we cannot leave. There seems to be no reason other than I must stay here and no amount of pleading seems to help.*

Heinrich Funks (Barbara's brother's family) *arrived here on Wednesday, October 13th, and hope to leave on Saturday. Oh, if only we and the children could travel together* (with them)*, that would make us so happy. Well, if God wills it.*

Saturday, October 16th. *The Funks left today. I have received the stamp from Dr. Hummel. Maybe I can leave with the children on Thursday.*

Thursday, October 21st. *We were all prepared yesterday. I do not think it will happen unless there is a great miracle during the night. In the morning I met Bergman and asked him to ask the authorities again for me. If they do not allow me to go and I have to remain here, who knows if we will all be together for Christmas. I looked so sad at times. Well, he* (Bergman) *asked and then he said, "Tante Neufeld, you have to wait for a little while. Can you be ready to leave in half an hour?" I was ready a long time ago. I was overwhelmed* (by the news).

Received the ship's pass. Had to sign and had to pay $15.00 and we were all so happy. We bought ten pounds of apples and a bit of cheese (Mundkäse). *Suddenly, just before evening, the agent said to me, "Frau Neufeld, you are not permitted to sail." Well, that's the way it goes. Nothing can be done. I went to see the doctor, but he pushed me out. "Go, there is no sense in talking and there is nothing that can be done." I insisted that Dr. Hummel had given us permission yesterday to go and I pleaded with him to let us go. We were not allowed to go because of Isaac and yet he has not been to see the doctor. He was healthy when we came to England. Gerhard was healthy as well. Only*

Heinrich had to see the doctor for four weeks and now we cannot leave because of Isaac? I have tried everything but to no avail. Suddenly everything looks so dark to me. I don't know how I will be able to manage with all the splitting headaches I have. I have at times had it so bad that I cannot describe it and cannot tell anyone about it, but I trust myself completely to a loving God. He will make all things well. He has never abandoned us even though at times it seems like God is not helping us anymore.

Hummel's stamp was not on the document and we were not allowed on the ship. I was comforted by the thought that we were being tested again. The others all went on the ship and we stayed back. The door was closed behind us and we were directed to go behind a high gate. We were questioned and examined and told no, no. We four stood there, all of us crying. How will it all end? We have to go back again. I pleaded and pleaded. Suddenly, Dr. Hummel with a smile on his face directed us through the door. He recognized us immediately and he had a brief conversation with Dr. Mengi. Then he said, "You can leave and board the ship." Oh, how my burden was lifted. Then I, together with the children, boarded the ship.

I realized now that he had taken my cabin number away, but the woman knew that the number was 745. We spoke with some people and were eventually told that the cabin was still empty. I slept that night as if I was in paradise. I gave thanks to God. I was so happy that I could not sleep. I cried for joy and said, "Dear Lord, take me as I am with all my children, here and in Canada, and those in Russia, all my friends and relatives and also our beloved who are still in England in Atlantic Park."

Frank Epp writes in *Mennonite Exodus*, "The detentions were a great disappointment to those involved. This was especially the case when a second rejection followed an initial release or if detention followed a successful passing of inspection."[47] By 1925 entire families were detained in Atlantic Park even if only one member of the family had a medical condition. That was because, if only one family member was detained, the others would appeal to the authorities on their arrival in Canada to have the detained family member released on compassionate grounds. By 1930 there were still six difficult cases of Mennonites who had been detained for seven years. Barbara and the boys were detained for over 14 weeks in Atlantic Park. It is surprising that the Neufeld children, aged 12 to 21, were allowed to proceed to Canada without detention and without their mother.

CANADIAN PACIFIC LINER "MELITA" 15,200 TONS

SS Melita of the Canadian Pacific Line

Friday, October 22nd. A very good beginning. We also received a very good meal. In the morning everything was inspected. The inspector walked around and made sure that everything was in order. We were able to stay in our room again which is so comfortable compared to the cold hard bed we had in England. Saw an island today with houses built on it surrounded by water. Our ship is called Melita, a beautiful ship.

Tuesday, October 26th. Saturday morning, I started to have headaches. Had them all day Saturday, could not eat for three days. Sunday morning it was a bit better, but I stayed in bed all day and then we got up for the meal and we also had breakfast on Monday morning, but then things got rough. The sea was very rough, so we did not need lunch or supper. Whatever was on the tables was swept off and many dishes broke. Then during Tuesday night and in the morning the sea died down a bit so that we could go and sit on the deck and then we went into the lounge.

Thursday, October 28th. It has been rumoured that today we will arrive in Quebec. We arrived in Quebec on Friday morning the 29th of October. Then we had to go through a long corridor until we came to a big room that was surrounded and secured by a fence where we had to wait again, but, luckily, we received our card and then finally our passport. When we completed the process and were ready to leave, they gave us a Testament (New Testament Bible). When we were ready to leave, Onkel Heinrichs from Pordenau asked me if he could help me. I gladly said thank you and he arranged for everything that we needed to purchase, two bags of food for three dollars. In the evening we left on the train. It was Friday evening, the 29th of October. We travelled all day Saturday and Sunday and arrived in Colonsey, Saskatchewan, on Monday.

Today is **Saturday evening the 13th of November**. Peter Voths came and got us from the station. It was November 1st and we had arrived safely, were very tired but happy that we no longer had to appear before the doctor. I can never thank Peter Voths enough for all the good that they have done for me. May the Lord reward them.

Early Days in Saskatchewan

On August 3rd I began to work for a farmer who lived north of the town of Viscount. It was, however, a bit early to harvest the grain so I had to do all sorts of other work. I could speak no English. I only stayed there for ten days, then Mrs. Voth said it was too far away, I would find work nearer to Colonsay. She phoned Mr. Schossling. He wanted a worker to set up the sheaves. (See box below.) **Mr. Schossling had a large farm that he had sold to ten Mennonite families. He had, however, kept three quarters of land.** (See box on p 94.) **He also had a worker who could speak some German. For Sunday**

Sheaves of grain were set up as stooks with six to eight sheaves placed together in a pyramidal formation. This was to shed the rain and to allow the grain to dry on the fields before being brought to the farm on hayracks for threshing.

I always came to the Gerhard Bergs where the rest of my siblings were. Peter and Anna had also gotten jobs working for farmers near Colonsay. Agnes was too young to be employed. After a few months, Mary came from Laird to Colonsay where she did housework for a farmer. I put up sheaves for Mr. Schossling for over three weeks, then I started to operate a threshing machine. The threshing was discontinued after the snow lay on the ground.

On November 1st Mother and the three boys came to Colonsay after having been in England for 3½ months. We were now all staying at the Gerhard Bergs. It did, however, not work well to have two women using one stove for cooking. We also tried to rent a house in the town of Colonsay but none was available.

Monday, November 29th. It is snowing hard today and it is very cold. All the threshing has been completed. The last stooks of oats were brought in yesterday. It is Thanksgiving here in Colonsay. There were a lot of guests in the church. Rev. Thiessen and Rev. Nickel led the service. On November 2nd we bought flour and sugar as well as lard and syrup and everything we need for meals.

Oh, if only God would help us soon in some way or other so that we might have our own home or house. Well, we want to trust the Lord who has taken care of our needs so far, and He has never forsaken us. He has not forsaken us during the famine or when He took our beloved Papa. He did not forsake me while I was in England while I was suffering there. He has always been near to us. To Him be thanksgiving and praise.

January 2, 1927. Johann and Peter have left for Alberta to look for something (a place to live). It was very cold a week before Christmas. The temperature varies a lot. Sometimes it is -31 degrees (Fahrenheit) and then it changes again. Then the weather was very nice on Christmas Eve. Here by Bergens there was a lot of company. The children said recitations and sang beautiful songs, some in English. The owner of this farm was not home. He and his family drove to see his brother who is very ill. He had bought something (Christmas presents) *for everyone, even for us. The children in school received a nice bag of treats and each child received a pencil. The bigger boys received a knife and the girls a kerchief. The adults in the family each received a cake. The school collected 35 cents for each child. All together each child received three bags* (of Christmas goodies). *Christmas Eve was celebrated on Wednesday in the school* (with a Christmas program). *The children drove there in the morning. It was very cold. They came home at 11:30 in the morning.*

Friday was Christmas Eve. There were a lot of guests for Christmas Day. The (church) *service was at Bergens. The adult choir also sang on the second day of Christmas. The service was at Toews'* (farm). *Here there was also a service on New Year's Eve (Sylvesterabend) as well as on New Year's Day.*

On January 6, 1927, Peter and I went to Kingman, Alberta. Jacob Loewens from our village in Russia lived there. They, however, were in the process of moving to Beaverlodge which is west of Grand Prairie. After a few days Peter returned but I wanted to travel with the Loewens to Beaverlodge to rent a house there. When Mr. Loewen and I wanted to purchase a ticket, the station agent told us that the train had not run for a time. The CNR had taken over this railway from the Northern Railway and things still had to be regulated. I then returned to Colonsay.

At home I immediately sat down and wrote a letter to Jacob Rogalski who was in Beaverlodge and who was my friend from Russia. He was to write whether there was a house for rent and, if so, we wanted to move there. He wrote back immediately that he had rented a house for us. We packed everything and moved to Beaverlodge, Alberta. (See box below.)

Edgar Rogalski writes of his father in a letter to me, "He was a sickly child [in Russia] and then the whole thing came crashing down with the Revolution and civil war. Yet he managed to finish high school in Ohrloff where his grandparents lived. He then had a year of agricultural school and another of teacher training. He made a couple of good friends in Marienthal, Jacob Thiessen, and Johann Neufeld. In fact, my Dad encouraged your Dad and the Neufeld family to move to Peace River from where they were staying in Saskatchewan. That was the beginning of the family connection with the Neufelds. We are so much the product of the intended and unintended journeys of our families."

We arrived by train in Wembley on February 3, 1927. That was as far as the train went. In Wembley, Johann Braul met us and took us to Beaverlodge in a box sleigh. We ate supper at the Johann Brauls, then Jacob Thiessen came and got us for the night.

Sunday, February 6th. We left the Gerhard Bergens on the 2nd of February and sat for four hours and drove (by train) *through the night until seven in the morning. Then we walked into a large building* (railway station) *and sat for a while, and then we walked to another station in Edmonton.*

We left Edmonton by train at 4 o'clock in the afternoon and travelled all night until 5 o'clock in the evening when we arrived in Wembley where we had to wait an hour. Johann Braul still had to work and then he came and got us. We drove for four hours but it was not too cold. We were bundled up in the sleigh and were nice and warm. Had to drive 23 Werst (15 miles) *until we arrived at Johann Brauls' for supper. Had Silfleisch* ("head-cheese," compacted ground meat from a hog's head), *fried potatoes, butter and white bread as well as good coffee with cream. It has been a long time since we had such a good meal. Then we were driven to Thiessens who took us into their house. The station where we arrived is Wembley. The town where we are renting lodging along with Abe Loewens for $10.00 per month is Beaverlodge.*

Beaverlodge in the late 1920s

Life in the Peace River Region

The next day we went to see the house Jacob Rogalsky had rented for us. It was a small house. The Abram Loewens lived on one side and we on the other. A stove was in it, otherwise there was no table, no chairs, nothing. We ate at the trunks we had brought from Russia and slept on the floor. Mother, however, cooked good meals and we were all well and happy that we were out of Russia. Mother has written in her diary how nice it is to live in a house by ourselves.

February 15th. On the 8th we came to our accommodation. Have a nice room that is big enough for all of us. (Barbara and eight children). *We also have a stove for cooking. It is so nice to have my own stove to cook on. The children are working. Hans goes every day and earns $1.00 a day. Maria works in the restaurant and receives $16.00 a month.*

February 25th. It was very nice for a week. Peter is working and receives $25.00 a month. Hans, however, does not have work every day.

Sunday, February 27th. The children were all at home except for Anna. She left yesterday evening for work (as a housemaid). *She receives $10.00 a month* (with room and board).

Beaverlodge was a very small town, not more than fifteen houses. At first, I worked for a Mr. Stevenson who did all kinds of work. He got wood out of the forest, that is, wood for stoves since everyone heated with wood. Mary worked for Mrs. Haladay who had a small restaurant. Peter began to work for a bachelor farmer. He did not like it there very much. At night the dog came and lay on the bed with him. He did not last there a very long time, then he looked for a better place of work. Annie worked for a farmer who lived somewhat further away from Beaverlodge. Mother then also did laundry for others. Agnes and the three boys went to school. We earned quite well, in our own way.

Mr. Stevenson did not always have work, so I began to work for Mr. Wilky, but he was a stingy man. He paid me $1.50 a day. When I asked him one time—it was spring already—if he could give me $2.00 a day, he was upset. I did not go back anymore. I then began to work for Mr. Clarence

Lawson, and I liked it there very much. I worked there all summer and long into the winter.

Already in Spring we bought ourselves a cow that we kept on the pasture of a farmer just across the fence from us. Also, soon after we came, we had bought beds, a table and chairs. In Fall we bought a sleigh and two horses. Peter and I wanted to get firewood out of the bush in winter. I had bought fodder for the cow and the horses from Mr. Lawson.

When possible, we went to the church service on Sundays. The Mennonites, approximately twelve families, gathered for services. They had services in the houses since there was no church. Jacob Thiessen was our minister. He had already been selected to be a minister in Russia and was ordained when the Hoffnungsfelder Mennonite Church in Wembley and Beaverlodge was organized. (See box below.) (In the photo of the church, is that Dad seated in the front row on the bench, third from the left? And is that Mom standing seventh from the right with Aunt Nellie standing on her left?)

Since most of our Mennonites were living on farms near Beaverlodge, we also investigated purchasing a farm. However, near Beaverlodge there seemed to be nothing available to buy. Aron Wiebe had heard that an Englishman, Nick Lingrell at Rio Grande, wanted to sell his farm with all that was with it—horses, cows, pigs and all the implements. Aron Wiebe took Peter and me there one day. We looked over the farm. The land looked quite good. The Red Willow River flowed right through that land. The yard and buildings were next to the river. The buildings—house and barn and hen house—were built of logs, all were in very poor condition. He had around forty horses he wanted to leave with the farm. Only six of them had been broken in, the others had not had halters on them. He also wanted to leave several cows with the farm as well as the pigs and chickens. The other quarter section was 2½ miles from this farm. There was some land on which we could plant grain; most of it was, however, not cleared, but also quite

The church building in Wembley was constructed in the winter of 1928-29 and made of logs from the nearby bush. In Beaverlodge a similar church was constructed on the farmstead of Jakob Thiessen. After he sold his farm and moved to Armstrong, British Columbia, the group met in homes.[48]

Hoffnungsfelder Mennonite Church in Beaverlodge, Alberta. [49]

good land. For everything he wanted $10,000. We did not have to make a down payment, but each year we were to make a payment with half of our crop. We were given fifteen years to pay for the farm. I think the interest was five per cent.

1928

Friday, February 10th. Hans and Peter have gone to look at a farm. We have bought a farm for $10,000. The first year the interest is 3% and then 6% so that it will be paid for in 15 years. The farm comes with 29 horses; 10 mares are in foal. Six beef cattle, three are to freshen, a drill, a binder, a plough, a harrow, a wagon, a sleigh as well as 45 chickens, and a house that is completely furnished. They (the Lingrells) *are taking the piano, a riding horse, and a car as well as the beds and their clothes. We signed the contract on February 14, 1928.*

We decided to buy the farm. On February 14, 1928, we bought it and on March 11, we moved there. We were quite pleased with the farm, except that it was so far away from Beaverlodge. It was twenty-four miles that we had to go to ship our grain in Beaverlodge. And on Sundays we had to drive those twenty-four miles with horses. Every second Sunday, when possible, we attempted to drive to the (church) services. (See box below.)

In 1928, the railway was extended from Wembley to the B.C. border. The railway went half a mile away from the small old town of Beaverlodge. Now a new town of Beaverlodge was built by the railway with six elevators and a whole street of stores, restaurants, and offices.

Mrs. Haladay also moved her restaurant from the old town to the new. Mary and Annie now both worked in her restaurant. Peter and I worked on the farm. Mother did the housework. Agnes, Gerhard (George), and Heinrich (Henry) went to school. Isaac began to go to school when he was six years old.

Thursday, March 31st. We bought a cow for $40.00. She is a good milker. On Monday we made soap. We bought 3 pounds of lye, the lard we got from Rogalskys. (Jacob Rogalsky worked in Smith's butcher shop in Beaverlodge.) It yielded very nice soap. The recipe for making soap is 5 pounds of lard, 1 red-pail of water, 1 pound of soda.

Sunday, April 22nd. It has snowed very hard for the past 14 days, but now it is very muddy, the snow is mostly melted away. We are to sow 50 acres of wheat and 50 acres of barley, and 20 acres of summer fallow needs to be ploughed. Thirty-two acres of trees need to be cleared.

In her diary, Barbara notes that they seeded 20 acres of wheat on May 7. There were six brooding hens sitting for about a week. By May 17th there were two foals and two more brooding hens. Fifty acres of wheat had been sowed. All the vegetables and potatoes were planted by May 16th. By May 26th all the Spring seeding was done including 50 acres of barley. By the end of May they had four foals, one mare and one stallion.

By the summer of 1928 the family must have owned an old car. Barbara Neufeld wrote in her diary, "Today is the 22nd of August. We went with our car to Beaverlodge to visit. It worked really well but now it is all broken." In 1929 she wrote, "Peter has gone to get the car fixed on April 19." An entry on May 11th continues, "We sold our old car, traded it in on a different one, had to pay extra."

We sowed wheat and barley, they grew well, and in the Fall we had a good harvest. Mother had her greatest joy in her beautiful garden and the chickens and young chicks. In Fall, when we were cutting grain, we had a lot of trouble with the binder. It was old, the grain had grown tall, and repeatedly we had to get repairs from Beaverlodge. One evening I said to Peter, "We can't go on this way." He should see if we could buy a different binder. At 2:00 o'clock at night he rode off to Beaverlodge. Early in the morning he had spoken to Mr. Lawson, the Massey-Harris dealer about getting a new binder. A new one cost $300.00, half of which we were to pay immediately. We, however, did not have the money. Since I had worked for his son Clarence Lawson the previous summer, he said he would loan us the $150.00 until Fall when we should pay him and the remaining $150.00 should be paid the following year. Peter bought the binder on this offer and at noon we had a new binder on the yard.

Sunday, July 22nd. The potatoes are all blooming already. Peter left on the 15th of July to help build a house for Funks on their homestead. Anna is home for 14 days. Now we have 93 chicks. Our first sow had 7 piglets on July 20th. One piglet was eaten by the other pig. We have already preserved 23 jars for winter—9 with just strawberries and 10 with strawberries and rhubarb.

August 5th. We have 118 chicks that have survived. The second sow has farrowed 7 piglets, the first had six. Yesterday Anna left again for the place where she is working. We have canned 50 jars for winter. The potatoes are big and we are eating them already.

August 22nd. We went with our car to Beaverlodge to visit. It worked very well, but now it is all broken. We started mowing (hay) *yesterday and mowed some today. We have had frost for three nights on the 20th, 21st, and 22nd. Each time it froze a bit more, but the cucumbers are not completely frozen. We have very nice wheat and very large potatoes, also very nice vegetables. The flowers are blooming beautifully, it is wonderful to see everything. We give God thanks for our health and blessings and for providing for us for the winter. It is a very warm day today. There have been very few mosquitoes so far. We have bought ourselves another stallion from our neighbour, a black one, for $50.00.*

On June 13th, Barbara Neufeld wrote, "The farm is better than I thought it would be." In the Fall she wrote a detailed description of a plentiful garden with a bumper crop of potatoes. "In my whole life we have not had so many potatoes." Further she writes, "...all together we have 1980 bushels of wheat and 1280 bushels of oats." These would have been very encouraging results from their first harvest on the newly purchased farm. In addition to providing food for the family and their animals, produce produced on the farm guarantied an income for payments for the farm and other necessities. Farm produce was also bartered for other necessities such as wood for heating the house. Barbara's diary is filled with details about activities and the resulting produce generated by the family's labour on the farm.

We harvested a good crop. In summer we had ploughed up sixty acres of unbroken land with horses and a plough and prepared the land for use the next year. In winter we had to haul the grain to the elevator. The next year—1929—we harvested 46 bushels of wheat to the acre; the price was also good. During the first two years we paid off $1000.00 each year on our farm. We could see that in ten years we would have paid for the farm.

1929

Wednesday, January 16th. *It started to snow on the first day of Christmas and it kept on snowing until recently, then it thawed. The girls* (Maria, Anna, and Agnes) *were all at home until after Epiphany, the 7th. Then we drove them all away again. John and Jacob Thiessen were here for a visit on January 13th.* (See box below.) *They came with the wagon. When they left to go home the snow was very deep. Now the snow is deep again, and it is still snowing. Tomorrow we want to take potatoes to Beaverlodge. We have already sold 25 bushels and now we are taking another 20 bushels as well as 100 pounds of carrots. Today we sold the foal.*

John Thiessen married Mom's sister, Susie Enns, and Jacob Thiessen married Maria. The close Mennonite community resulted in many marriages of young people whose families knew each other through their shared history in Russia and the church they attended.

Monday, March 11th. Heinrich Funks (Barbara's brother) *were at our place today. They came on the 9th of February* (March?) *and left on the 11th. Today Peter and Johann went to haul logs that they cut down for the chicken coop.*

Monday, March 24th. The weather is still nice. Everything has been shipped. To Lingrells, 1238 bushels. We kept 540 bushels for ourselves. We get about 20 eggs each day. Everything is dry. We brought Lingrells two sacks of potatoes in exchange for wood.

Sunday, March 31st. We received a letter from Greta.

Barbara regularly corresponded with Greta, her daughter in California, and with her sister Elizabeth Wichert. Although Barbara visited with relatives and attended church services, weddings, and other functions of the church community, she often writes of her loneliness without a husband and living far from Beaverlodge.

Sunday, April 21st. I have already read Bible stories to the children; this is the only good thing for me on this earth. I feel very lonely and forsaken, and at times I feel left out. When will the time come when we will be there with all the devout ones and we will see each other again?

1930s: Hardships and Weddings

Then came the 1930s when there was almost no money. The depression was suddenly upon us. Instead of getting $1.50 per bushel of wheat as in the previous two years, we now received 18 cents per bushel of wheat, for oats we got 5 cents per bushel. A good milk cow cost $10.00 and a 200-pound hog only $2.00. I went to Mr. Lingrell and told him that half of the crop that we shipped would be put in his name but that he would get very little money for it. We simply could not pay off anything on the farm. He was very good and said he wanted to have nothing. We should, however, try to pay the taxes so that he and we would not lose the land. The taxes were $12.00 per quarter section of land, $24.00 for two.

Many who worked at some employment away from home could not find jobs. They had to have government aid and that was very little at that time.

For us, however, the good Lord provided in that we could live on a farm. We always had enough to eat. In Fall, we took fifty bushels of wheat to a mill in Sexsmith. We had the wheat ground and had enough flour for a whole year. We butchered hogs and a cow and had enough meat. Milk, butter, and eggs we had, also everything that we got out of the garden. Housewives, and also our mother, were resourceful. For whatever could not be bought a substitute was found. The most difficult years were 1931 to 1933.

February 28, 1931. We had company on Sunday. Both girls came home and then Jacob Thiessen and Jacob Rogalski came. We talked about engagements with the two girls, Maria and Anna: Maria with Jacob Thiessen and Anna with Jacob Rogalski. They have known each other for a fairly long time and have asked me for permission which pleased me greatly.

I feel so close to my beloved children that the Lord has entrusted to me not so very long ago. I have to think of all that has happened during this time. My wish and my prayer are may God go with them and bless them at the beginning (of their lives together). *May the Lord bless them on their life's journey in good times and in hard times, and that the Lord may bless them* (the two Jacobs) *in our family, that we might get to know each other and overlook each other's shortcomings with love.*

March 16th. We celebrated the engagement at our place on the 14th of March. Mr. Thiessen presided over the engagement. I had a severe headache, but it let up in the evening. We felt especially blessed to have such nice weather. The next day, the 15th of March, the young people came to our place, they sang and played games.

April 20th. We went to Beaverlodge on Good Friday but there was no Holy communion. (No communion because no *Ältester*—Elder—was present to give the sacraments. See box below.) *We were received as members of the congregation; me, Hans, and Maria.*

In the Anabaptist/Mennonite tradition, Ältester was the highest, most responsible position in the church, roughly equivalent to that of a bishop as mentioned in Acts 14:23 and 1 Timothy 5:17. (The elders who direct the affairs of the church well are worthy of double honour, especially those whose work is preaching and teaching. 1 Timothy 5:17.)[50] Only an Ältester could perform sacraments such as baptism, communion, and marriage within the congregation.

On June 1, 1930, Mother, Mary, and I joined the Hoffnungsfelder Mennonite Church, and Peter and Annie were baptised that year. (See box below.)

On the 22nd of June there was a baptism in Beaverlodge. Elder Harder officiated; there were seven baptismal candidates. Our children, Peter and Anna, were also baptized as well as Nela and Justina Klassen..." (Peter and Nela were married a year later.)

1931 was a special year for our family. My sisters Mary and Annie both were married on April 12; Mary to Jacob Thiessen and Annie to Jacob Rogalski. The wedding was on the farm of the Jacob Thiessens in Beaverlodge. These were the parents of Mary's bridegroom. And my brother Peter married Nellie Klassen on June 26. The wedding was also on a farm at the Klassens since at that time we did not have a church building. All services, including Sunday services, were in homes.

April 21st. "...I stayed at the Funks for 14 days until the 2nd of April, then I came with Jacob Rogalski to Beaverlodge to Thiessens and then we prepared for the wedding that was at Thiessens. I baked bread and Zwieback and cooked meat on the 12th of April. I felt quite well, things went better than I had imagined. The bridal couples arrived on the last day of Easter, the 6th of April, and we baked a lot of cookies. We butchered a hog for the wedding and then we all drove to Beaverlodge on the 12th of April 1931. They were married by Jacob Thiessen. The preachers were G. Neufeld and Johann Schmidt. They received many gifts at the rehearsal party (Polterabend).

In the Mennonite/Anabaptist tradition, baptism was a solemn rite entered only by choice on confession of faith and usually by young people in their teens. Baptism was followed by first communion, a holy sacrament together with other church members. Membership in the church was granted concurrently with baptism. Because Barbara, Mary, and Hans were baptised in Russia, they were also able to join the Hoffnungsfelder Church in Beaverlodge.

Front Row: Maria & Jacob Thiessen; Henry, Isaac, and George Neufeld; Anna & Jacob Rogalski. Back Row: John, Agnes, and Peter Neufeld

Already in the previous Fall, 1930, the Jacob Enns family had moved to Beaverlodge. Once in winter, when a service was at the Jacob Löwens (they had a log house on their yard in which the service was held) on that evening when we had youth club (Jugendverein), I saw Louise (Liese) Enns for the first time. (See box below.) I wondered if the dear Lord would be able to guide the two of us together. I prayed about this. And God also wanted that. We didn't know, however, that we still had to wait eight years.

Liese (pronounced Leezuh) is a diminutive form of Elisabeth in German. When Mom arrived in Canada, she didn't want to be called Elisabeth, so she had her name changed to Louise in English. In Appendix 2, the *Canadian Board of Colonization* document lists her name as Elisabeth on her arrival in Canada.

Before Peter's wedding in May, Peter's fiancé, Nellie (Nela), and her parents visited us one time. As Mr. Klassen and I sat outside for a bit after supper, he suddenly said, "Well, now is soon the election for elder and minister and then they will elect Neufeld's Johann as minister." I now knew that the people were thinking of choosing me as minister.

Nomination and Ordination to Ministry

Now a little about the Hoffnungsfelder Mennonite Church. In 1926, a group of Mennonite immigrants at Wembley bought the Adeara Ranch and another group at Beaverlodge bought the Ralph Carol farm. Other Mennonite families at Wembley and at Beaverlodge bought other farms. People came together at both places on Sundays for services. In 1927, the two groups wanted to unite as a congregation. Already in February 1931 this congregation had decided to elect an Elder from their four ministers. This election was to be held on June 27. It had also been decided to elect some more ministers. (See Appendix 5, page 195, for more information on the Adair farm and the Hoffnungsfelder Mennonite Church.)

My brother Peter's wedding day was on June 26. Elder C.D. Harder of Rosemary, who had been invited to conduct the elder and minister election, performed the marriage of Peter and Nellie on Friday, June 26. Then on June 27 the election for Elder was held first in the home of Jacob Löwen since Beaverlodge had no church building. The vote for Elder fell on Jacob Nickel. Then ministers were elected. Abe Peters of Wembley had the most votes, then Jacob Friesen and me.

Friday, July 10, 1931. The wedding was on the 26th of June. It rained so that the guests had to leave after the noon meal but toward evening the weather became nice again. The speakers at the wedding were Jacob Thiessen, Beaverlodge, and Dietrich Weibe from Brainard. Ältester (Elder) Cornelius Harder officiated at the wedding ceremony. After Faspa, Gerhard Neufeld (Adair Ranch) and Jacob Nickel from Brainard spoke. Hans, Isaac, and I drove to the wedding in Mr. Norman's car. The two, Gerhard and Heinrich, also came to the rehearsal evening (Polterabend). *There were many guests and they* (Peter and Nela) *received many gifts. May the Lord bless them in our family and may they feel welcome. Papa* (Barbara's husband, Johann) *would really have liked to be here at the wedding, yet, if he were asked, he probably would not want to come back. May the Lord allow us to all meet again where there is no separation, where our joy will be complete.*

On the 27ᵗʰ of June there was a vote for Ältester led by Ältester Cornelius Harder, and Jacob Nickel was elected. There was also a vote for minister and the following were elected: Peters from Adair Ranch, Jacob Friesen, and our Hans.

On the 5ᵗʰ of July Peter and Nela came to our house; both were very happy. Maria and Jacob Thiessen were also at home and they are very happy. They took two horses along to break up land and Peter took his things, his bed with bedding, and a sack of wheat for his piglet. He will be living with his in-laws until he has something of his own.

Nela Klassen and Peter Neufeld

On Sunday, June 28, we had a baptismal service in the forenoon and communion during the afternoon. After communion, when we were standing outside in the yard, a minister of the Krimer Mennonite Brethren Church who had also been at communion came to me and greeted me as minister. He encouraged me; I should consider taking on that work. Then soon after that, a man of the Mennonite Brethren Church, also having been at communion, came and said he had prayed that the vote would fall on me and, before we drove away, Jacob Enns, who was to become my father-in-law eight years later, greeted me as minister. On December 13, 1931, I preached my first sermon, and on August 6, 1933, I was ordained as minister by Elder C.D. Harder.

After their wedding Mary and her husband Jacob Thiessen moved to a farm, first near Beaverlodge and then to a farm at Goodfare. Annie and her husband, Jacob Rogalski, moved to a homestead near Lymburn and Peter and Nellie stayed in Beaverlodge. At first, he worked for a farmer and then later at the experimental farm.

Thursday, December 31st. The three, Johann (Hans), Heinrich and Gerhard have gone to get firewood and brought back a big wagon load. We have Christmas behind us. We all went for Christmas Eve and for Christmas Day services. Our Hans gave the sermon as well as J. Friesen and Jacob Thiessen. We feel very fortunate. On the second day of Christmas we all came to our place. We had a very good Christmas. We even had a nice Christmas tree.

We butchered a hog one day before my birthday and then all the children were home. They helped a lot and then they all went home on the 16th of December (Barbara's birthday). *I have "shrunk" a lot this year* (meaning the family got smaller with three children being married). *I received an iron from Peter and Nela for my birthday and a pair of stockings for Christmas. From Gerhard I received a white bowl and a wedding picture from Anna and Jacob. I also received a picture from Peter and Nela. The pictures are very important for me.*

Sunday, January 10, 1932. Until now it has been good skating weather but now it looks like it will thaw. The three youngest (Gerhard, Heinrich, and Isaac) have good skating and we three are at home (Barbara, Hans and Agnes).

Here ends Barbara Neufeld's diary. Edgar Rogalski, who translated her diary, writes, "The little booklet started by her late husband (Johann Neufeld) was full at the beginning of 1932. I suspect that she must have written more but it was lost."

Many of the pages of the diary (not quoted here) are filled with everyday notes about the weather, people, events, farm animals and produce. Barbara does not mention the financial difficulties the family experienced during the Depression of the 1930s. She was a mother with deep faith in the "will of God" to guide them through daily life and the difficulties of pioneer life in the Peace River region of Alberta. Her faith sustained her through the death of her husband, single parenting eight children, emigrating from her homeland, and resettlement in a new country.

"Grossma," Grandma Barbara Neufeld as remembered by her grandchildren.
(The cap she wore was to relieve her headaches.)

A Farmer and a Minister During the 1930s

I continued to work for Mother on the farm at Rio Grande. It was very difficult on the farm because the Depression continued. We could not pay off debts on the farm. One year after the other this happened. In the years 1930 to 1934, the only thing that had gone up was the interest on the farm debt. We, that is, Mother and I came to the decision that we wanted to return the farm to Mr. Lingrell, the owner. Also, we thought the time had come that we needed to move closer to our Mennonite Fellowship. For me as a minister, it was better if I was closer to a Mennonite group. When I spoke to Mr. Lingrell of it in the spring of 1934, I said I wanted to return the farm to him. If he wished to pay me something for these years in which we had worked on the farm I would be grateful and, if not, I would also be thankful. Then he said, "Oh no, you have worked hard on the farm." The land was very much improved, he would repay us plentifully. On April 10, 1934, we terminated the main contract. He, however, gave us eight horses, almost all the cows and calves, the hogs, and chickens, and almost all the farm implements except for the plough and the wagon. The plough we also did not wish to have. We were very thankful. He was very good to us. We rented the farm for two more years.

In 1936, we left the farm and moved to Lymburn. In a book I wrote down that in eight years we had threshed 16,541 bushels of wheat and 9,287 bushels of oats. If the Depression had not come, we would have paid for the farm, not in fifteen years, but in ten years.

Already in the spring of 1935 we bought a quarter section of land near Lymburn for $400.00. It had been a homestead but was now already a farm. On November 23, 1935, we moved from Rio Grande to Lymburn. Now we were closer to a Mennonite fellowship. Here there was a church in which a service was held every Sunday. I was here for only one winter from November 23, 1935, to April 1, 1936. Mother's sons, George and Henry, were now grown up. I thought they could take over the farm and look after Mother.

It was around this time that Rev. Jacob Thiessen of Beaverlodge moved to B.C. That group was now generally without a minister. Jacob Friesen, who was elected as minister at the same time as I was, did preach there but did not want to undertake all the work. I was asked to come to Beaverlodge to serve this group.

Mr. Elias Smith was looking for a worker. Mr. and Mrs. Smith were both old people; he was over seventy years old. He had a small farm of forty acres near the old town of Beaverlodge, he had about a dozen milk cows and sold the milk in the town. He also had land in other places that he rented to others. This man wanted to have a worker. I took the position for the wages of $10.00 a month as well as room and board. My living quarter was a bunkhouse on the yard. I began to work on April 1, 1936.

On Sunday, I served the group with the Word of God and sometimes also during the week on an evening meeting if it was desired. Now I recognized that I was badly in need of biblical knowledge. Soon after I was called into the ministry, I thought very much about going to a bible school, perhaps in Winkler, Manitoba, where the Mennonite Brethren church had one. However, during the Depression, that opportunity was completely impossible. I could at that time also not leave Mother and my younger brothers alone on the farm. When I, on one occasion, spoke of this to an older man in the congregation, he said to me, we very much need you here now. Books that could be of help I had very few of, and an actual Bible commentary not at all. I wrote to Pastor Ernst Modersohn in Germany to ask whether among his *Heilig dem Herrn* subscribers there might be those who would be willing to send me old copies of *Heilig dem Herrn*. (See box below.) I did then receive more than ten years' worth of copies that helped me very

---

In 1906 Eric Modersohn began a popular publication titled *Heilig dem Herrn: Wochenblatt für Jedermann* (Holy to the Lord: Weekly Paper for Everyone). Rather than a scholarly publication, it was essentially an inspirational commentary on biblical passages for the average reader. After 1910 Modersohn became the most prominent evangelist in Germany, but during World War II he was considered a traitor to the regime and imprisoned by the Gestapo. After several weeks he was released but he was forbidden to travel and speak or write publicly.

much. However, I only got them in 1940 after the war with Germany had begun.

During those three years that I served the group in Beaverlodge with the Word of God, I had difficult hours but also very many happy ones. Only a few examples: It was difficult when I, as a young minister, had to counsel married couples who had strained relations, but the joy came in seeing that almost all the people came whenever they could to the services. We had our worship services in the homes because we had no church building.

It was once during the first week of January when we had prayer meetings on three evenings that it had snowed all day before the meeting. I thought on this evening no one would come. I didn't want to go but in the last few minutes I decided that I would go. I had no horses with which to travel. I walked in very deep snow for 2½ miles. When I arrived, most of the people were already there, some having come twelve miles with horses to participate in a one-hour prayer meeting. In the room it was already warm. There was a table behind which I stood, the congregation before me, behind me was a window that was completely frosted over. Because I had walked in the deep snow, wet with perspiration, I stood there the whole evening and shivered. The congregation paid close attention and quite a number took part with prayers. To this day I do not understand how it was that I did not become ill. The dear God protected me against illness.

Mr. Smith was a good old man, but his wife was not good. She could not get along with people, particularly not with the women who came to work for her. At first, Mr. Smith delivered the milk in the town himself, then he hired someone to do that. Once he hired an old man, but he stayed with the work for only three months because he was an alcoholic. Another time he hired a young man eighteen years old. His name was Herb Wagner and he was from Elmira, Ontario. He told me that he had been confirmed that year. He was Lutheran. Often, in the evenings in the bunkhouse when I read the bible and prepared myself to preach, he said, "Give me your hymn book." Then he would find hymns such as *A Mighty Fortress is Our God* and sing them with a loud voice. These were also happy hours for me.

On April 17, 1936, my sister Agnes married John Thiessen of Goodfare. They moved to a farm near Goodfare but later moved to one near Lymburn.

Neufeld Family at John and Agnes' wedding
Standing, L to R: Peter, George, Jacob Rogalski, Agnes, John Thiessen, Jacob Thiessen, Isaac, John, Henry. Sitting: Nela (Klassen) Neufeld, Anna, Barbara, Maria

Courtship, Marriage, and Years of Difficult Work

Louise Enns knew for a while that I had my eyes on her. It was in the summer of 1937, on a Sunday after the worship service, that the Peter Neufelds and Abe Wienses wanted to drive to the Jacob Friesens for dinner. They asked Nick Enns who had a car if he would take them there. Nick Enns was willing to do that. They also asked me if I wanted to go along. It happened that I had to sit in the front of the car next to Louise. As we were driving, Louise suddenly placed her hand on mine. I knew what that meant. When we all returned towards evening, I stayed at Louise's place for supper. Nick drove to Wembley to get his parents who were visiting there. On this occasion, I asked Louise if we might be able to walk the path of life together. At that time, she could not yet make up her mind. Only after our wedding did she tell me that reason: she thought being a minister's wife was too great an assignment for her. (See box below.)

In November 1937, I ceased working for Mr. Smith. Since I did not want to leave the group at Beaverlodge, I had room and board with my brother Peter Neufeld. That winter I read a lot that helped me further my work for the Lord.

In 1938 it was very dry in Beaverlodge. It did not rain for a long time, and since people were just barely out of the Depression, there was little work to be had. The money I had saved during my employment was coming to an end. I paid Peter Neufeld $10.00 for room and board every month. However, during harvest time I wanted to earn something. I heard that there was a good harvest in Tofield. At the beginning of August I travelled to Tofield by train. I found work 6 miles north of Tofield setting up stooks for Mrs. Seal. For three weeks I set up stooks. On Sundays I went to Jacob Kliever's where I always experienced friendly hospitality. When I had finished stooking for Mrs. Seal, I began to work with Lesley Maginite's threshing machine. Mr. Maginite lived west of Tofield. We threshed until late in the Fall. Afterward, I worked at various other places until November 25. On Sundays, I was now at Peter Penners' who were also very good to me. During this time, I preached in the Tofield Mennonite Church several times.

I had written to my brother Peter that I would come back late in November. When I arrived in Beaverlodge by train, I saw that someone of every Mennonite family was there to see if I had arrived. That was a fine welcome. I again served that group with the Word of God. On Christmas Eve the children presented a nice program.

Mom told me several times that she had said to Dad she could not be a farmer's wife due to a chronic illness from her early childhood. She felt that she was simply not strong enough to meet the demands on a farm. These may have been concerns she expressed to Dad in addition to those about being a minister's wife. It is apparent that Dad did not pursue a vocation as a farmer after their marriage as did most Mennonite pastors. He took great care of Mom during the many years she suffered from arthritis often massaging her arms and legs to relieve her pain. She was later also diagnosed with fibromyalgia.

1939 was another special year. On January 6, the Abram Löwens wanted to have a thanksgiving celebration. Their little son had come home from the hospital, healed after having been there for thirteen months. In Fall they had raked leaves on their yard and had lit them. The little boy, I think his name was Peter, had fallen into the fire and his legs were somewhat burned. The doctor had taken him to the hospital immediately and he was healed and released only after thirteen months. The parents were so happy that they now wanted to have a thanksgiving celebration. Several families drove out to this celebration on that day. I went along with the Johann Brauls. We had a service there. I preached on Mark 1:40, "Lord, if you will, you can heal me." In this case, the Lord had wanted to heal Peter.

After the service we all had dinner and visited until 4:00 in the afternoon. Then we drove back home. One mile from Beaverlodge, Johan Klassen with whom I was travelling, turned off to drive his parents' home. I got out to walk this mile. Louise Enns also got out. We both went to Beaverlodge. While walking she asked me why, since my return from Tofield, I had not come to them. I sometimes say that this was the hour in which we knew that we belonged together. During the following weeks we did see each other now and again, and on April 9, we were engaged. Since that was exactly on Easter, Elder Nickel had come to Beaverlodge for the Easter service. In the morning he had an Easter sermon and during the afternoon he had a short message for our engagement. Exodus 33:15 was the scripture on which he spoke. "If your presence does not go with us, do not send us up from here." It was such a suitable text for Louise and me.

After Easter I got a letter from Cornelius Toews of Wembley. He asked if I would be willing to come to Wembley to serve them with the Word of God and to take over the work in that group. Frank Jansen and Gerhard Neufeld who had been ministers there had moved to Vauxhall one month earlier. Abram Peters, who had been elected minister eight years earlier when I also was elected but who had yet not accepted, now also began to preach. Cornelius Toews wrote that I could work for his son Peter Toews. He urgently needed a worker. I agreed to do that and worked until one week before our wedding. Peter Toews was at that time not a Christian but later converted and became a sincere Christian. In this time, between Easter and our wedding, I walked eighteen miles several times to see my bride.

On August 6, 1939, we had our wedding. It was exactly six years earlier on August 6, 1933, that I was ordained. Elder Jacob Nickel of Lymburn performed the marriage ceremony. The biblical passage which he chose was Matthew 23:8. "For you have one teacher, one is your master, Christ." Elder C.D. Harder, who was holding bible discussions in our congregation, was also at the wedding. He had the opening sermon on Peter 4:8-10. The wedding was in the Mennonite Church north of Wembley (that was then known as the Ranch). Many guests had come from Beaverlodge and Lymburn and probably all who lived in Wembley as well as many of the Mennonite Brethren Church in La Glace.

The church was completely full. The choir from the Mennonite Brethren church sang beautiful hymns. The reception was a simple lunch, and everyone stayed for it. Later the choir sang some more beautiful songs and Mr. Hoepner had a short message. In the evening after this beautiful day, Louise and I thanked our loving Lord that He had led us together and prayed that He should also help us further.

Peter Enns, Louise's brother, had a farm close to the church. He wanted to have a worker on his farm until the winter. He was a truck driver. We took up this offer and lived with them in their house.

Above: Louise & John Neufeld (Log church in background?)
Below: Louise, John, ?, Freda Fast

Neufeld Family

Adults: Maria, Anna, Jacob Rogalski, Barbara, George, Louise, John, John Thiessen, Henry, Agnes, Isaac, Peter, Nela.
Children: Erna Thiessen; Herb, Werner, and Victor Rogalski; Irma Thiessen; Walter and Cornie Neufeld

Enns Family
Standing: Frieda & Nick, Margaret & Cornie Fast, Annie & Peter, Louise and John, Freda Fast. Front: Margareta Enns (with Bill Enns), Jacob Enns. Boys: Arthur & Arnold Fast, (Edwin Enns, head)

Before I continue about us, I would like to mention something about Louise's parents and background.

Louise Enns's Family (See first box below.)

Louise's Grandfather, Nikolaus Enns, was born in Russia in 18?? (birth unknown). He married Katharina Schroeder or Abrams. (Nick Enns has written Schroeder in a family history, whereas Louise and her sister Susie say that her maiden name was Abrams.) Grandmother Enns was born in 1846. We could not find out when they were married. The Lord granted them three children. Jacob (Louise's father), Sarah, and Katharina. Grandfather Nikolaus Enns died in (?). Until Grandfather's death, they lived in the village of Paulsheim—not Paulsheim but rather Gnadenheim. Grandmother then married again; I do not know in which year. Her husband was Johan Martens. They moved to the village of Eliesabetthal where they had two more children, Johan, and Nella. Grandfather Martens died in 1919 or 1920.

Grandmother Martens, at the age of 48 or 49, was very ill for a lengthy period. She had to stay in bed for almost a year. She had earnestly prayed about her health and had made a vow to the Lord. If the Lord would make her well again, she would enter his service. And the Lord answered her prayer; she became well again. When she was well, she sent for books on midwifery and on herbal medicines and was able to help many sick people. Into old age she worked as a midwife. In over forty years she was present at 1420 births. (See second box below.) Hospitals and doctors were very few so

---

A family tree compiled by Eleanor Kasdorf (nee Enns) gives the following account of the origin of the Enns name. "The name Enns is said to have originated from the River Enns in Austria. During the time of the Reformation, in the early part of the 16th century, two small boys were found on the banks of the river Enns. One died of exposure. The survivor was too small to give any information about himself except that his name was Abraham. So, he was named Abraham von der Enns. All the Ennses are said to be descendants of this Abraham. The above information was arrived at before the First World War by two independent investigators." The fact that the independent investigators are not identified leads one to wonder if this is another family myth that may have grown from a kernel of truth.

If Grandmother Martens was 48 or 49 at her illness, she would have been a midwife for over thirty years rather than for over forty years when she died at age 82.

for births one always sent for a midwife. Most of the women whom Grandmother helped were Mennonite, but there were also Russian women and gypsy women. Never was it too much for her. If someone came to get her, she went along, even if it was at midnight. The women who were approaching delivery needed to be helped. With gypsies in their tent, where there was no bed and the woman lay on a blanket on the ground, Grandmother knelt and helped with the delivery.

Once when she was in our house, perhaps it was at the birth of my brother George, as she walked out the door where I stood, she laid her hand on my head and said, "And you are also one of my boys." Grandmother Martens died in 1928 when she was a little over 82 years old.

Katharina Martens and adopted Russian daughter

Now I will write a little about her children. I will write later about Jacob, my Louise's father.

(See **Appendix 4, page 193,** for "Grandmother Martens'" children, the siblings of Jacob Enns (Louise's father), and the Russian daughter that she adopted.)

Now, of Louise's father.

Jacob Nickolai Enns was born in the village of Gnadenheim on August 8, 1870. He moved to the village of Eliesabetthal with his mother when she married Johan Martens. In the village of Alexandertal, he learned the craft of painting. He was a painter. When he was twenty years old, he was baptized on his confession of faith and became a member of the Pordenau Mennonite Church. Here he got to know Margaretha (Greta) Isaak. She was the daughter of Johan and Sara Isaak of Pordenau. They, however, moved to Samara when the Samara settlement was founded. Father, Jacob Enns, also travelled to Samara and on November 19, 1891, these two, Louise's father and mother, were married.

Grandfather Isaak was seven years old when he immigrated with his parents from Prussia (Germany) to Russia. Where they lived at first, I do not know, perhaps in Pordenau. Grandfather's second wife was Sara Unruh. His first wife died and left him with three children, Johan and two girls. The one married (?) Janzen and the other one died. Johan Isaak, the son of Grandfather, lived in the village of Pordenau. He had a very nice farm. I learned to know him there. He died of typhoid in 1919.

Grandfather and Grandmother Isaak had seven children, five girls and two boys. Mother (Greta) was the oldest. I have already written that she married Jacob Enns. Then was Maria who married Heinrich Nachtigal and lived in Samara. Liese was the third one. She married Heinrich Sukau and also lived in Samara. He was a missionary among the Russian people. He had done much work for the Lord. During the communist regime he perished in exile. Jacob died when he was sixteen years old. Sara married Heinrich Derksen of the village of Hierschau. Anna married ? Toews and later lived in the village of Waldheim. And David, the youngest, married Liese Schroeder. Of all of these, Mother emigrated to Canada, and her youngest brother David, during the Second World War, came as far as Germany where he died in the 1940s.

Grandfather Isaak was a minister in the Mennonite Church in Samara. When they were old, the Isaaks came back to Pordenau and lived with their son Johan. Grandmother Isaak died in 1913 and Grandfather died in 1916. I can remember seeing Grandfather Isaak in the Pordenau Church when he was a very old man.

Father and Mother Enns were in Samara one year after their wedding, then they moved back and initially lived in the village of Eliesabetthal and then they moved to the village of Pordenau. At first, they lived on a small farm (*Kleinwirtschaft*) near the church. (Later, Jacob Penner— Reimerpenner—lived there.) Then Father and Mother Enns bought a complete farm in the east (end of the village) on the south side of the street in the village of Pordenau. Johan Isaak, Mother's brother, lived across the street.

Enns house, barn, and Nebenhaus (adjoining house) in Pordenau.

The Lord granted our (Louise's) **parents fourteen children.**

- **Johan Enns, the eldest, was born on June 17, 1893, and died in 1895.**
- **Nikolai was born on August 15, 1894, and died in 1897.**
- **Katharina (Tien) was born on September 3, 1896. She married Jacob Toews; their wedding was in September of 1919. They had two children, Gerhard and Jacob (Jack or James). Gerhard died as a small child and Jack or James came to Canada in 1926 with his mother who had remarried. During the Second World War, James was in the army for several years.**

Jacob Enns was born on March 8, 1898. He married Maria Heinrichs of Pordenau on May 13, 1919. Maria Heinrichs was born on May 21, 1899. They emigrated to Canada in 1926. At first, they lived in Watrous, Saskatchewan, then they moved to Armstrong, B.C. and then to Campbell River, B.C., where they still live today. He is 77 years old and she is 76. The Lord granted them eight children. Katharina died as a child and Mary married Victor Fast. Jake died when he was in the army at the age of twenty. George died when he was two years old. Walter married Ruth Allison and Rita married Ernie Vliet. Edward is married to Lorraine Hoover and Gerald to Susie (?). They all live in B.C.

Then was Sara Enns who was born on July 6, 1899. She married Corny Wall, the neighbour's son in Pordenau, on March 31, 1919. Corny Wall was born on February 23, 1897. They emigrated to Canada in 1926 and have probably lived in Watrous, Saskatchewan, the entire time. Sara died in 1954. Corny Wall remarried on September 23, 1956, with Mary Janzen. In 1958, both died in an automobile accident. She died immediately and he a few days later. The funeral of Corny Wall was on September 25th and his wife's funeral was on September 20th.

Corny Wall and his wife, Sara, had ten children.

Jacob was born in August 1920 and died in 1921. Margaret was born on April 4, 1922. She married John Klassen and lived in Oliver, B.C. They have two sons. John Klassen died in 1967 in Oliver. Margaret then married Fred Rempel. It was an unhappy marriage. John Wall was born on October 6, 1923, and married Hedy Toews. They have three children. The John Walls live in Watrous, Saskatchewan. Katharina (Katie) was born on February 27, 1925. She married Henry Dick and they live in Winnipeg, Manitoba. They have four children. Frieda was born on June 25, 1929, and married George Janzen. They have three children and live here in Calgary. Erna was born on October 13, 1931, and married Clarence Jantzen and they have two children. They live in Saskatoon, Saskatchewan. Irma was born on October 19, 1934, and married Kenneth Thompson. They have four children and live in B.C. Anne was born on July 23, 1936, and married Edgar Dick. They have five children and live in B.C. Lillian was born on November 7, 1938, married Irvin

Koop and they have three children. They live in Winnipeg. Velma was born on November 3, 1941. She married Walter Penner and they have four children. They live in Lethbridge, Alberta.

Margareta was born on February 27, 1901, and died soon after that.

Johan Enns (Hans) was born on March 24, 1902. He married Liese Toews. The wedding was on the 10th of (?) in 1924. Soon thereafter he was conscripted into the Russian state service. Because he was a committed Christian, he did not take up arms and had to suffer much because of that. When the Mennonite emigration began, he was in the service. His father did not want to emigrate at that time, but Johan had written again and again that they should emigrate. He and his wife would also emigrate as soon as he was dismissed from service. Because of his continuous writing, Father and the entire family decided to emigrate. When he had completed his state service, Russia had closed its doors to emigration so that no one could emigrate any longer. It was probably in 1932 when he was among the first to be sent into exile. There he starved to death in 1933. When his father and mother, then living in Beaverlodge, heard of it, Mother had been very dejected. She had begun to weep loudly and to cry; why did her son have to starve to death. His wife, Liese, moved during those difficult years to the settlement of Stavropol where she soon also died. (See box below.)

Nickolai Enns was born on February 18, 1904, and died as a small boy in 190(?).

In the periodical *Atlantic*, Anne Applebaum writes that the government under Stalin in 1933 convinced the Russian people, through massive propaganda, that those people who lived in the Ukraine were not "human." She quotes Lev Kopelev, a Soviet writer who had served in an activist brigade in the countryside as a young man. He too had found that clichés and ideological language helped him hide what he was doing, even from himself. Kopelev wrote, "I persuaded myself, explained to myself. I mustn't give in to debilitating pity. We were realizing historical necessity. We were performing our revolutionary duty. We were obtaining grain for the socialist fatherland. For the five-year plan."

continued ...

Of the propaganda and the awful famine caused by Stalin's five-year plan that resulted in 4 million deaths in the Ukraine, an area that included the Molotschna Colony, Applebaum continues to write, "There was no need to feel sympathy for the peasants. They did not deserve to exist. Their rural riches would soon be the property of all. But the kulaks were not rich; they were starving. The countryside was not wealthy; it was a wasteland. This is how Kravchenko described it in his memoirs, written many years later:"

> Large quantities of implements and machinery, which had once been cared for like so many jewels by their private owners, now lay scattered under the open skies, dirty, rusting and out of repair. Emaciated cows and horses, crusted with manure, wandered through the yard. Chickens, geese, and ducks were digging in flocks in the unthreshed grain.[51]

It was during this time that John Enns was transported to Siberia where he died. Mom's account of John's exile was that only two or three people survived in the railway boxcar transporting them to Siberia in the harshest conditions of overcrowding. Those individuals were later able to get word back to relatives and friends.

In 1929 the Canadian Mennonite Board of Colonization desperately sought admission for 1,000 Mennonite families facing deportation to Siberia. The Saskatchewan government refused them outright, as in turn did other prairie provinces. Eventually about 1,300 Mennonites were able to enter, mostly settling in Ontario. [52]

Johan Enns and Liese (Toews) Enns

127

Margareta was born on December 20, 1905. She married Corny Fast. The wedding was on December 29, 1928. Corny Fast was born on May 18, 1902. At first, they lived for several years in Cereal, Alberta. Then in the 1930s they moved to Beaverlodge where Corny worked at the Government Experimental Farm. In 1943 or 1944 they moved to Ryley next to Tofield. They lived there only a short time and then moved to Chilliwack, B.C. where he worked at an army camp (I think, as a secretary) until he retired. Presently they live within the city of Chilliwack. They have three children. Arthur was born November 13, 1929, and married Dorothy Funk. Frieda was born on January 28, 1931, and married George Jong, and Arnold, born on February 24, 1934, married Viola Funk. Then the Fasts had adopted a daughter, Rita Sawatsky, who married Henry Voth. All the children live in B.C.

Peter was born on November 20, 1907. He married Annie Kaethler. Their wedding was on July 29, 1933. Annie was born on June 18, 1912. For quite a few years they lived in Wembley, then in 19(??) they moved to Tofield, Alberta. They have seven children. Edwin was born on April 11, 1934, and married Erna Boese. (See box below.) Maria was born August 4, 1936, and died soon after. William was born on October 3, 1937, and married Louise Walde. Verna was born on January 27, 1940, and married Oscar Epp. Rita was born November 20, 1942, and married Dennis Hoveland but they have separated. Aron (Arnie) was born on September 19, 1945, and married Deanna Hildebrand, and Walter was born on April 20, 1948, and married Clara Larson. All the children at present live in Edmonton except for Walter who lives in Grande Prairie.

Susie was born on November 25, 1909, and married John Thiessen. Their wedding was on April 21, 1933. He was born on November 14, 1905. After the wedding, they first lived in Beaverlodge and then moved to Oliver, B.C. and then in 196(?) to Chilliwack, B.C. They are retired now. They had three children. Hilda was born June 11, 1934 and died soon after birth. Louise was born June 19, 1935, and married John Goertzen, and Margaret was born February 9, 1938, and married John Peters.

Erna's first husband, John Wall, died when a combine fell on him while he was repairing it.

Maria was born in 1910 and died in 1913.

Nikolai was born January 12, 1913, and married Frieda Braul. Their wedding was on July 7, 1939. Frieda was born March 28, 1919. They also lived in Beaverlodge and then moved to Gem, Alberta, and then to Chilliwack, B.C. where they now live. They have four children. Edward was born May 14, 1942, and married Deanna Turchak. Eleanor was born January 25, 1944, and married Arthur Kasdorf. Phillip was born May 14, 1946, and married (??). Lillian was born March 20, 1950, and married Chris Bartel.

Louise, of her I have written that we had our wedding on August 6, 1939. She was born in the village of Pordenau, South Russia, on March 1, 1916.

Members of Enns family at emigration.
Liese (Louise), Nickolai, Margaretha (Isaak) Enns, Peter, Jacob Enns, Susie, Margaret

Early Years in the Beaverlodge Area

I have already written of our wedding, that after the wedding we lived with Louise's brother, Peter Enns. To go on a honeymoon after the wedding was an opportunity one could not take at that time since I did not have much in the way of material goods and Louise did not have much more. All that I had was a small chest with my clothes and books. Louise had her clothes and bedding and then also a sum of travelling debts which had not been paid at the time when she came to Canada. (See box on p. 130.)

The "chest" to which Dad refers is a small hand-made wooden container, 14½ x 24 inches by 12 inches deep, with a handle and a latch. I don't recall Mom and Dad ever measuring happiness or success in terms of accumulated things or wealth. My memory is that they lived a life of gratitude for the little they had. Dad was committed to providing just enough for his family without being distracted from his work in the church by striving for material gain.

Our wedding was on Sunday. On Monday bible discussion was still held in our church, and on Tuesday Peter Enns showed me how I should drive his tractor and that I should check that it had enough oil. Then I was to plow the summer fallow. Until that time, I had never driven a tractor. He then drove his truck (freight) to Edmonton and only came back after several days. Everything went well with the tractor.

After a few weeks, Louise's parents also moved to the Peter Ennses. After Louise had married, it was too lonely for them in their house in Beaverlodge. Peter had a large log house, but for three couples it was a little close.

On workdays I worked for Peter Enns while he was trucking, and on Sundays I served the group (the congregation) with sermons. Abram Peters also helped. Louise and I, and also others, soon noted that evangelism was necessary. Louise and I prayed about it and suddenly, without our doing anything, an evangelist, Heinrich Verner was his name, came and wanted to hold meetings in the church. He was permitted to do this. He was a Baptist.

Already on the second evening, when the invitation for a decision was made, several people stood up. He bade them come to the front. Since they hesitated, I also stood up and bade them come to the front. We wanted to pray with them. Several young people came forward and took Jesus as their Saviour. Also, on the following days several more came. Unfortunately, those from the Brethren Church thought all the new converts would join their church. I thought differently and prayed that the Lord would make known his will here, which he also did. Those whose parents were from our congregation remained with us, and those whose parents were of the Mennonite Brethren Church joined that church. These evangelistic meetings were just a week before Easter. After Easter I had catechetical instructions for six or seven persons and on Pentecost, Elder Nickel baptized them.

Peter Enns had another small log house, 14 x 18, on his yard. The Hans Bekkers lived in it, but they moved out in Spring and we then moved into it. That was quite wonderful, to live in a house by ourselves, and Louise cooked the best of meals.

In summer Louise told me that the good Lord wanted to grant us a baby. We anticipated it with great joy. Yet, before it was to arrive, we had to live through two major events.

Even before our wedding Louise occasionally experienced appendicitis. On September 19, 1940, she again had an inflammation. She was very ill. I went to the neighbour, Norman Anderson, and asked if I might borrow his Model T to take Louise to the doctor in Grande Prairie. He let me take the car and we drove there that same evening. The doctor admitted her to the hospital immediately. It was already high time that she should have an operation. At night they had already applied ice. In the morning the hospital phoned that I should come to give permission for the operation. I went with Peter Enns to Wembley, then took the train to Grande Prairie and, once there, went immediately to the hospital. When I arrived, I saw them wheeling Louise out of the operating room. I spoke to the doctor. He said they could not have waited until I had come. After two weeks I could take her home, but the doctor suspected, and we also, that the birth could be premature. Louise's operation was on September 20th.

Exactly one month later, on October 20th, it was a Sunday morning, Father suddenly came very quickly to us and told us that Mother was very ill and we should come. We left our breakfast and went immediately. Mother wanted to get from the bed to the chair. Peter and I helped her. We noticed then that she could no longer speak. She had had a brain hemorrhage (*Gehirnschlag*). We laid her on the bed in the large room. She was now already unconscious but breathed until 1:00 o'clock when she drew her last breath and went over into eternity. Louise's mother was dead. Since at that time it was not yet the custom for an undertaker to look after the dead body, Heinrich Goerzen made the casket the next day and the funeral was on October 25.

We phoned the Nikolai Ennses and Cornelius Fasts immediately and they came even before Mother died. Corny Walls from Watrous, Saskatchewan, and the Jacob Ennses and John Thiessens all came to the funeral. Corny Walls came via the train and, since the train was somewhat late, the funeral was also an hour later; instead of at 2:00 it was at 3:00. Louise and I were not in the church at the funeral. Because of the imminent birth, we did not trust our going. We did, however, go to the cemetery that was close to the church. As the sun set, the casket was lowered into the earth. Mother reached the age of 66 years, 10 months, and 5 days. She had been married with Father for 48 years and 1 day. Elder Nickel had the sermon at the grave side.

Jacob Enns, Louise's brother, went back to B.C. the day after the funeral. Corny Walls and John Thiessens stayed on and wanted to visit for a couple of weeks. At first, they visited at Wembley (Ranch) for a week, then they drove to Beaverlodge to visit the Corny Fasts and Nick Ennses. Louise thought that the time for the birth would soon be upon her when she would have to go to the hospital in Grande Prairie, but she wanted to see her siblings once more before they travelled back home.

The fifth of November, I went right after dinner to ask the neighbour, Norman Anderson, if he would lend me his car again. He did that willingly. So Louise and I drove first to Beaverlodge. We had some car trouble on the way. The brakes on a front wheel braked (unexpectedly?) from time to time, yet we did get to Beaverlodge. I left Louise at the Corny Fasts where her other relatives were, and I took the car to the garage. They inspected everything, cleaned the brake, and I could again drive. We stayed at the Cornie Fasts for only an hour, then we drove off to Grande Prairie. It snowed, the wind got stronger, and the snow was beginning to drift somewhat. We got to Grande Prairie without incident. I left Louise with the Peter Schroeders. They were older people, and they often took in women who had to wait for delivery.

Now it had gotten dark. I drove back. The wind was driving the snow even more and it was cold. I left the car at Norman Anderson's and walked the remaining 1½ miles home. The house was cold, the windows frosted up, I made a fire in the stove and warmed myself thoroughly. Then I lay down to sleep.

On the following morning, around 10:00 am, the Ennses had the radio on. After the news there was an announcement that a little before 9:00 am our Linda was born. The Ennses came and told me the news right away. I was happy and thankful that God had led my taking Louise to Grande Prairie the day before since in the night, with the wind and snow, it would have been very difficult to take her there. As soon as I could I drove to the hospital in Grande Prairie.

Louise told me then that she had gone to sleep peacefully at 10:00 pm at the Peter Schroeders and at 5:00 in the morning she had phoned Dr. Carlael who had come and had taken her to the hospital. Linda had arrived a little before 9:00 am. That was on November 6, 1940. It so happened that another woman that Louise knew well from Beaverlodge also had a baby. Her husband had come in the morning and was so overjoyed at the birth of his baby that he had gone to the CFGP radio station and had the arrival announced over the radio. At the same time, he had announced Linda's birth. That is how we heard it over the radio. On November 18th I brought Louise and our Linda home. (See box below.) At home, when our Linda cried or screamed, it sounded as if she was calling "Mam." And so I will not continue to call Louise by her name but rather Mam. (Mam is a short form for Mama in German.)

And Linda did not want to eat or drink the first few days she was at home. Then Mam sat and cried. But when Linda noticed that one could not live in this world without eating, she began to drink her milk. Now she was our complete joy.

Two days after Linda was born, on November 8th, the Corny Walls again returned to Saskatchewan and took Father along. That was, on the one hand, good for the Peter Ennses and for us. However, for Father it was a great mistake that he was making. First, he was very homesick—lonely for his wife, our Mother, who was in the grave—but also for the others with whom he had always been together.

A twelve-day stay in the hospital after giving birth was not unusual during the 1930s and 1940s.

In the little house at Peter Ennses in which we lived, we had various experiences. Once at night, when it was extremely cold outside, Mom put the hot water bottle in Linda's bed so that she should stay warm, but in the middle of the night, she took Linda and put her between us. She slept in warmth, but in the morning, we saw there was ice in the hot water bottle.

We were rather poor at that time. The group (the congregation) had agreed to pay me $10.00 a month as their minister. If we had received that, we could have bought the bare necessities to some extent, but they had declined so much during the depression that they could also not pay us the $10.00. Once, we had no flour for baking and no money to buy it. Mam and I prayed earnestly about it and a miracle happened. While we both were not at home, someone had put a hundred-pound sack of flour in our house. To this day we do not know who did that, but we thank God that He answered our prayers.

Peter Enns, Mam's brother on whose farm we were living, now had enough work with trucking so that he did not want to continue renting the farm. Peter Spenst then rented the farm. Peter Ennses, however, wanted to continue living on the yard. They wanted to move into the little house where we lived since it was their house. To where should we move? The congregation (the group) gave advice. They would buy logs and I was to build a house on the churchyard about twenty steps from the church. The logs that they bought at the sawmill were cut logs, 4x8 inches thick. They were made as tongue and groove. The house was 14x18 feet big. I mitered the corners nicely. There was no foundation under it. The roof was just of boards. The floor was of boards. There was, however, no ceiling in it. On April 2, 1941, we moved into the house and Mom made it as beautiful and pleasant as possible.

Then on May 16, Father came back from Saskatchewan. Where should he stay now? At the Peter Ennses, who lived in the little house where we had lived earlier, it was too crowded. He then came to us and lived in our house.

I was able to find very little work to earn some money. In May, John Harder came (he was also a Mennonite—had once belonged to a Mennonite

Brethren Church, but no longer) and asked if I would help him dig a hole for a basement, 24x28 feet. His farm was 2½ miles from where we lived. I was willing to help him for one dollar a day. I did a lot of digging and he removed the earth with two horses. When we had the hole ready, I alone put up the basement forms. He himself sat inside most of the time. When I had done that, I asked if he had a cement mixer with which to pour the basement. He said, "We don't need one. I will get enough workers to mix it by hand."

On the next day, exactly one boy came and helped until the following noon when he said he had to go play ball. So, I was left by myself to do the work. For three and a half days I mixed the cement by hand (that is, with a shovel) and then shovelled it into the forms. What a job that was for only $1.00 a day.

One day in July our neighbour Peter Spenst came and asked if we would like to go to Tofield with him. However, he set a condition: I was to drive his car, a Model T. We were willing to take up this offer. Mam's uncle and aunt, the Jacob Klassens from Beaverlodge, had already moved there the year before, as did my brother Peter with his family. Mrs. Spenst who was not very well did not want to go along, so their daughter, Mary, and Herman Wall came with us. On July 10th we drove off. At Faust, a little place near Slave Lake, we stayed overnight in some cabins and on the following day in the evening we arrived at my brother Peter's place near Tofield. He lived on a farm that he had bought. We visited in Tofield for a week and then drove back without having had any problems. We had been away for eight days.

The next day Johan Harder came again and asked if I would build the house for him. He had logs cut 4x8 inches (tongue and groove). I consented and built the house for him. I had to miter the corners very well. I did not know how to cut the rafters. For them he hired John Nickel. I nailed the roof with boards and shingled it with cedar shingles. Since the farmers were now beginning to cut their grain, I wanted to earn some money putting up sheaves. I asked Johan Harder if he could pay me. He said he had no money; I was to wait. He then did pay something but the final amount he paid a week before Christmas. With the setting up of sheaves at Pete Epp's and with threshing, I then earned some money.

Life in Tofield

Since it was going a little better for the farmers, many thought to move to another location where farming would be somewhat easier and where they could join a larger spiritual fellowship (*Gemeinschaft*). From Beaverlodge, half of the Mennonite families had already moved away and from the group at Wembley (the Ranch) there was also talk of leaving. We also began to think of moving to another place. My brother, Peter, wrote that we should come to Tofield. We sold the little we had, the rest we packed, and on April 1, 1942, we took the train to Edmonton and then to Tofield. The congregation or group had a farewell celebration for us. Abe Peters, who was doing more of the preaching, now took over the work in the congregation in Wembley for a short while.

After two years, most of the group at Wembley had moved away. From Beaverlodge, all the Mennonite families moved away, so also most of the church members at Lymburn. Elder Nickel moved to Rosemary.

Mom's father also moved with us to Tofield. Peter Neufeld got us from the train, and we stayed there for ten days until our things that we had sent as freight arrived.

In the town of Tofield we rented a small, very low house (shed). (We just couldn't get anything else.) We moved into it and Father with us.

David Thiessen, who had also moved from Beaverlodge to Tofield, had bought a farm near the town. He wanted to hire me to change the windows in his house. This I did for 25 cents an hour. That was quite a good amount that he paid.

I heard that Boyd Stauffer wanted to build a new house on his farm. I went to him and asked if he could use another worker. He said "yes" and hired me for 35 cents an hour. Joe Burkholder was the foreman. I was very happy that I could work here. From Mr. Burkholder I learned carpentry and I decided to be a carpenter.

Before I continue, I want to write a little about my siblings and their children.

I wrote that on April 12, 1931, two of my sisters, Mary and Annie, had weddings on the same day. Mary married Jacob Thiessen and Annie, Jacob Rogalski.

Mary and her husband lived for some years on a farm near Beaverlodge, then they moved to a farm near Goodfare. In 1946 they sold that farm and moved to a farm (an irrigation farm) near Rosemary. In 1974 they sold this farm and built a house in the little town of Rosemary. They are retired. The Lord granted them six children. Erna married Henry Ratzlaff and lives on a farm near Rosemary. Anne married Cornie Voth and they live on a farm near Beaverlodge. Alma married Herman Lepp and lives in Harrow, Ontario, on a fruit farm. Herman is also a minister in the congregation. Mary married Denny Smith. They live in Winnipeg and Denny is a dentist. Mary was a registered nurse (R.N.). Bernie married Kathy Sawatsky. He is a high school teacher in Rosthern. Donald married Evelyn Wiebe. They live in Steinbach and Donald is a teacher.

Annie, my sister, and her husband, Jacob Rogalski, moved after their wedding to a homestead near Lymburn. On this homestead that soon became a farm, they lived until 1942. At the beginning of March, they sold this farm and moved to Vineland, Ontario, to a small fruit farm. On January 25, 1974, my sister Annie's husband, Jacob Rogalski, died and the funeral was on January 28th. We also went to the funeral.

The Lord granted them six children—five sons and a daughter. Herbert is married to Lorna Dyck. They live in Vineland, Ontario. Herb is a janitor in a school. Victor is not yet married. He lives at home and works for another farmer. Werner is married to Louise Andres. They live in Vineland and he is a mechanic. (See box below.) Edgar is married to Carol Enns and he is a teacher. They live in Hamilton. Paul is not married. He lives at home and is employed away from home. Laura is also not married. She is a registered nurse (R.N.). She was in voluntary service in Haiti for two years.

"Vineland" should read "Virgil" where Werner was a mechanic for many years.

137

Peter, my brother, of him I have already written on page 105 that he married Nellie Klassen on June 26, 1931. After the wedding they lived for a year with the Klassens. Then they moved to a house that belonged to Ed Heller, a farmer. Peter worked for him on the farm for several years. Then he began to work on the experimental farm near Beaverlodge. They built a small house in the old town of Beaverlodge. Here they lived until 1941. They sold what they had and then moved near Tofield on a farm. Here they farmed until 196? when they sold the farm and built a house in Tofield into which they then moved. Peter then did carpenter work for several years. He is now retired.

The Lord granted them also six children—four sons and two daughters. Walter, the eldest, is married to Selma Regehr. They live in Tofield. For many years Walter worked for the Crown Lumber Company in Tofield. Presently, he is a contractor and builds houses in Tofield. Cornie married Noreen Williams. They also live in Tofield. He is the oil agent in Tofield. Arthur is not yet married. He lives in Edmonton and works at a business for Groser Parts (machine parts). Erna is married to Walter Braul. They live on an acreage near Edmonton. He is a lawyer. Elsie is married to Allen Reichenbach. They also live in Edmonton. Elmer is married to Jennifer Matter. They live on an acreage near Edmonton.

Agnes, my sister, married John Thiessen from Goodfare on April 17, 1936. I have written about this already on page 114. After the wedding, they moved on to John's homestead near Goodfare. Here they lived for several years and then moved to a farm near Lymburn. In 1947 they sold their farm and on January 17th moved to Tofield. Southwest of Tofield they bought a quarter section of land and later they bought another quarter section. They are still living on this farm.

The Lord granted them four children, too—three daughters and one son. Irma is the eldest and is not married. For many years she worked in a bank in Edmonton. At present she is living at home with her parents. Betty married Al Jerke. They live in Edmonton. He has his own business doing a lot of work with cement. Johnny is married to Lois Koop. Their wedding day was on July 4, 1977. Verna is married to Arnold Wiens. They live in Edmonton and he is a truck driver.

John and Agnes Thiessen retired from the farm in the summer of 1977. In the town of Tofield they built a house and moved into it. When John Thiessens moved to Tofield in 1947, Mother, George, Henry, and Isaac also sold the farm in Lymburn and moved to Tofield. Initially they lived with the John Thiessens, then however, Mother and George moved to Ontario. Isaac had already gone earlier to work there. Henry went to B.C.

In 19?? Henry married Elsie Franz in B.C. in Abbotsford. He had already gotten to know her in Tofield. In B.C. they lived near West Abbotsford where they had several acres of berries. In 19?? they sold these acres and moved to Tofield. Southwest of Tofield, just south of the John Thiessens' farm, they bought a farm. Here they lived until 1973 when they sold the farm and moved into the town of Tofield where Henry built a very nice house. He now works mostly at the Crown Lumber in Tofield.

The Lord granted them three children—two daughters and a son. Velda married John Munsma. They lived here in Calgary. He worked for the government. Velda became ill, and on June 26, 1975, she died. The funeral was in Tofield in the Mennonite Church on June 30, 1975. Linda married Dave Goretzki. They live in Edmonton. Donald is not married. He took his training in a technical school and works in Edmonton.

Mother, George, and Isaac returned from Ontario in 195?. Mother stayed with my sister Agnes and her husband John Thiessen.

Isaac, my brother, married Neta Regehr of Ryley on November 14, 1954. They bought a house and several acres of land north of Tofield and lived there until 19??.

They also have four children that the Lord granted them—three daughters and a son. Debbie is not married. She attended the bible school in Swift Current and at present is working in Edmonton. Diane went to bible school and is also working in Edmonton. Nancy is still attending school as is Melvin.

George, my brother, lived for several years in a trailer at my brother Isaac's after he and Mother returned from Ontario. Most of the time he was employed, most often with construction work on a highway. Here he also

139

had a stroke in 195?. He was in the hospital in Grande Prairie for a time, then he came to live with my brother Isaac in his house for the rest of his life. After the stroke he was lame. He could only walk very slowly, and his left hand was paralysed. His voice was very weak. It was hard to understand him. In 1962, George participated in the catechism instructions and on June 10th I baptized him. He was the first person whom I baptized. In 1969, in June, my brother George died, and on June 28 was his funeral. I gave his funeral sermon. We siblings were very grateful to Isaac and Neta that they had looked after him so many years.

Mother, after returning from Ontario, lived the rest of her life with Agnes and John Thiessen. During the latter years, she also had to be cared for almost completely. Her memory also became weaker during the last years. On January 28, 1965, she entered into eternal rest. The funeral was on February 1st. She became old with 82 years, one month and 11 days. Mother and brother George are both buried in the cemetery near Tofield. Two gravestones stand there for them.

Of Mom's siblings I have written earlier.

In the little shanty in Tofield where we lived at first, we stayed only for a few months, then we rented the house next to it. This was the last house on the street. It was also small but at least it was a house. A small barn was also with it. Mr. Hockedall, a farmer who was also an elevator man, lived in the town of Tofield. He asked if we would look after a cow for him. We could have all the milk and butter for that; he only wanted to have us bring him two quarts of milk each day. We were willing to take his offer. At the railroad there were several acres of land that were fenced in but that no one used. In summer there was a good pasture there. We were permitted to take the cow to the pasture there.

I wrote earlier that I began to do carpentry work for Boyd Stauffer. Joe Burkholder was building the house for Stauffer. When we had completed this, I was out of work. A mile south of the town of Tofield, there was an open coal mine. Quite a few men worked there. Some worked only a half day. These men earned more for a half day than I did when I did carpentry work for a full day. I then wanted to work there too, but I worked there only half a day. Then I realized that the work was too hard for me. I have never gone back to work there.

In the town of Tofield stood an old two-storey office building with a high tower. This was to be demolished and a new one was to be built of the wood. A contractor from Edmonton had the contract. I again got work as a carpenter with him. When this was done, I did various jobs or all kinds of work that I could get. In winter I also shovelled much snow for others.

In the congregation I was also drawn into the work. There were eight ministers, but because I was an ordained minister, I was also to serve here with a sermon now and then. Even before we had joined the Tofield Mennonite Church, there was a brotherhood council meeting (*Bruderberatung*) at church on a Sunday afternoon. We had gone along to visit at the Jacob Klassens when some who had been present at the meeting also came there afterwards. They told me that the congregation had elected me as a Sunday school teacher. Now I again had work in the congregation every Sunday. For four years I was a Sunday school teacher. This work went quite well for me. After four years I was elected as superintendent of the Sunday School. In this position I worked for eight years. In Fall of 1942 we had joined the Tofield Mennonite Church as members. Mom began to help in the Ladies' Aid.

Mom's father, who was living with us, had suddenly bought two lots of land south of the Mennonite church in March and told us that he wanted to build a house there. He said that in two weeks we had to get out of this house. That was completely new to us. That produced misunderstandings because I had rented the house and had paid the rent. Also, I said that a house had to be put on a foundation and had to have a small cellar. Both could not be dug in March because the ground was still frozen.

It was in May when I dug a cellar, 8x8 feet and 6 feet deep. The earth was so hard here that it took me 3½ days to dig it with a pick and shovel. It was very warm and there were an awful lot of mosquitoes. Here I came into such temptation that I threw down the spade and walked away. Only my love for Mom and our little Linda didn't allow that I . . .

When I had finished digging the cellar, I dug very little for the foundation. Because very little cement could be bought, the forms for the foundation were made very low, only one foot high. Jacob Friesen brought some sand and so with a shovel we mixed cement by hand so that it should be well compacted. With this work the nail on one finger was injured somewhat. When I was painting a picket fence in the next few days, I got blood poisoning in that finger. My whole arm was swollen up. For two days I had great pain. Then I took the bus to Edmonton to a doctor. (In Tofield there was no doctor at that time.) In Edmonton Dr. Twilinger looked at the finger a long time, then he sent me home, telling me to hold the hand in very hot salt water and in two days I was to come back. Then he would operate on the finger.

On June 1st I went back to Edmonton, I had to go to the Royal Alexandra Hospital immediately, and on June 2nd I had surgery on my finger. I was in the hospital for four days, then I came home again. After a few days someone came from the Crown Lumber Company to have me come to pile up boards. I went but had to be very careful because of the finger. When after a week I returned to the doctor to have the stitches removed, I told him that I had already worked with that hand. He said that was entirely the right thing to do since otherwise my finger would have gotten stiff.

One day when I came home from work, Mr. Burkholder was at our place. In the previous summer I had worked for him when we built Boyd Stauffer's house. He asked if I wanted to work for him again. He had undertaken to build a house for Menno Widemann. I was willing to do this and had work until the fall.

Father then all alone built the house, 16x26 feet, south of the church.

We already knew that our Arnold wanted to come to us. On September 24, 1943, I went along with Mom on the train to Edmonton. Dr. Law put Mom in the Misericordia Hospital immediately and on September 25, at 6:30 in the morning, our son Arnold was born. That Saturday I was again working at the Crown Lumber Company. The hospital phoned there immediately. That was a great joy for me. When I told our neighbour V. Krul that we had a son, they said they wanted to take me and Linda there, and right on the following day. It was Sunday. When I saw Mom in the hospital, the first thing she said was, "Now we have a real family, a daughter and a son." When I then looked through the window of the infant room, I saw our Arnold for the first time. I saw that he turned his head and looked at me as if he wanted to see, "and who has come now?" Mom and I were overjoyed and thanked God that our son was a healthy, strong boy. We accepted him as a gift from God.

On October 2nd, somewhat earlier than we had expected, Mom came home on the bus with our little Arnold. Mrs. Krul who had seen Mom coming down the street with her bundle had gone to meet her. She looked into the bundle and said, "Mrs. Neufeld, that is not your baby; they have given you the wrong baby in the hospital." Mom, however, insisted that it was her baby and that she would never give it away.

Linda was particularly happy that Mom was home again. During the time that Mom was in the hospital I had taken Linda to Mrs. Kliever every morning and had gotten her in the evening. She didn't want to go there at all. In the morning she would scream when I went there with her. She was happy when I got her in the evening.

Daniel, Linda, and Arnold in front of the "little house on the prairie"
that Grandpa built. (An outhouse, a chicken coop and the garage can be seen
in the background with a swing in between.)

When Father had shingled the little house and had put windows and doors in it, he went to Oliver, B.C., to John and Susie Thiessen. When he returned, he wanted to sell the house for $325.00. We were willing to buy it for that price and paid for it monthly. I then finished the inside with plaster board (gyprock) and then, on October 15, 1943, we—I, Mom, Linda, and Arnold—moved into our house. To this house we added twice; the first time in 1953 we built a kitchen and in 1967 we added six feet for a washroom when running water was brought as far as our place. We lived there for 30 years. On December 1, 1973, we moved to Calgary.

The first extension built in 1953 with a kitchen and a boys' bedroom. In the background, a hen house, garage, and 1949 Plymouth(?) car.

Father also lived with us, but in August 1944 he again went to B.C. to Oliver where he wanted to stay at John and Susie Thiessen's for a longer while. In July 1956, Father came back from B.C., and on May 18, 1957, he died at our place. The funeral was on May 22nd in the Mennonite Church in Tofield. He was buried north of Wembley where Mom's mother was buried.

A white fence and Russian poplars were added later. (Some of the trees were still there in 2022.) Dad was red-green colour blind, so Mom and I painted the house yellow and aqua-blue. Werner Rogalski, Mom, Louise Rogalski. (Photo 1965)

Second extension with bathroom and entry built in 1967.

Previously, I have written that, in the year 1943, I helped Menno Widemann build his house. Then the next year I helped David Heidebrecht, who had moved into the house where we previously lived, to make the house larger and rebuild it completely. It was probably on July 7th that lightning hit the house, but the fire was put out on time. Then the next year I already built on my own, first a house for my brother Peter on his farm, and then for others. So I mainly did only carpenter work now.

When our Linda was a little over three years old in 1944, I think in February, she became ill. She had a high fever. Since there was no doctor in Tofield at that time and we did not have a car, I asked my brother Peter Neufeld to take us to the doctor in Holden. The doctor immediately said that we should go to Edmonton to a doctor. When we drove back, we stopped in Ryley at Cornelius Fast's and asked him if he would take us and Linda to Edmonton on Monday. He was willing to do that. On Sunday, Linda became very sick, and when we got to Edmonton on Monday, we found Dr. Law was not at home, but Dr. Jesperson said right away that Linda had rheumatic fever. He had her admitted to a hospital immediately. We brought her to the Misericordia Hospital.

When we returned after a couple of days, Dr. Jesperson said that Linda needed to have a blood transfusion. Since the war was still on, there was no blood bank for this hospital. We were to give the type of blood that Linda had. The next day a whole carload of people (from Tofield) drove to Edmonton to give blood, but no one had the type that Linda had. In the following days quite a number of people drove to the hospital, but no one had the type of blood that Linda had. After three weeks Linda no longer had a fever so Dr. Jesperson said we could take her home. However, if she should be ill again, we should bring her back again. So, we took her home.

After a month she became ill again. It was the day after Easter that we took her to Edmonton. Now Dr. Jesperson put her in the Royal Alexandra Hospital. In this hospital there was a blood bank, and they had the type of blood Linda needed, however, in return someone was to give as much blood as Linda would use. While we were sitting in the waiting room Mom talked to a woman who also sat there, and she told her our problem. She said that every month her husband gave blood to the hospital. In ten minutes, he would come to the hospital. When he came, the woman talked to her husband who then went immediately and gave blood. We wanted to pay him, but he took nothing, would not even give his name and address. Linda became well and, after a week, we could take her home. Dr. Jesperson feared that her heart might have been damaged from the fever. Linda, however, was well and became a healthy, strong girl. So, God answered our prayers and made Linda well.

The terrible Second World War that began on September 3, 1939, ceased in 1945. Everywhere people were glad and rejoiced that peace had come again.

In 1946, the loving God again wanted to give us a great gift. Now it was Daniel whom he wanted to give to us. Already earlier, Mom had asked, "What will it be, a boy or a girl?" Whatever the good Lord would give us, we would accept as a gift from Him. In Tofield there still was no doctor and no hospital, so I had talked to our neighbour, Jacob Kliever, about taking us to a hospital in Edmonton. He already had a car whereas we did not have one yet.

On February 19th it was a cold windy day. In the evening, Mom said to me, "We may have to go to Edmonton this night." And, in fact, at night Mom suddenly said, "Now is the time." Our neighbour, Jacob Kliever, who lived in the caretaker's house next to the church, was willing to drive at night. I left Mom in Edmonton at the Misericordia Hospital and went back home with Mr. Kliever. I had just had the flu. When, on the following day, February 20th, I took the bus to Edmonton and came to the hospital, Mom told me that our son Daniel was born at 5:00 in the morning. This boy also was a healthy, beautiful child. We thanked God for this gift. We were poor, but the loving God had made us wealthy in that He had now granted us three healthy children. On February 27, Mom and Daniel came home.

1949 was the year in which the loving God had another special blessing for us. He had granted us three children and He had supplied all our needs. Now, to the three children, He wanted to give us one more. Now we had a good doctor in Tofield, Dr. Freebury, and a good hospital had also been built.

Mom, however, was not very well this time. On September 20th, I took her to the hospital and at 10:20 pm our son Gerald was born. On the following morning, before I drove to work, I went to the hospital. The nurse said that we had a healthy, husky boy. It was, however, breakfast just then so that I did not see Mom. When I finished work, I went right to the hospital. Mom felt quite good and we were both happy that this child also was a healthy, normal child. We thanked God also for this gift that He had granted us.

Linda now also went to school and we were happy that she learned well. At home, as the oldest, she thought she had to look after her brothers. She believed that she was already somewhat responsible for her brothers.

Arnold, Linda, Dan, Gerald (in front) with the Grade 1 school on the left and the roof tops of other single classroom schools and a large brick school in the background on the right.

School for Grade 1 built in 1903.

School for upper grades. Its interior was gutted by fire in 1958 after which the outer structure was demolished .

Tofield schools in 1967, the year of my graduation.
Round building, junior high school, grades 7 – 9.
Central building, elementary school, grades 3 – 6.
Building on the right, senior high school, grades 10 – 12.
Connecting the latter two was a gymnasium.
Grades 1 & 2 were in separate one-room buildings
that were moved from surrounding districts to the school grounds.
(Partly visible at the right in the photo.)

Ministry and Work in the Tofield Mennonite Church, the Conference of Mennonites of Alberta and the Conference of Mennonites in Canada

I have written that right from the beginning when we came to Tofield I was drawn into the work of the congregation, first as a Sunday School teacher and then after four years as superintendent of the Sunday School. Right from the beginning we noticed that there were two parties (groups) in the congregation. That sometimes led to small misunderstandings. Only much later after many years, when the younger ones were drawn into the work of the congregation, did this disappear completely.

In 1943, David Heidebrecht was ordained as elder, but in 1948 it was his wish that one of the other ministers should take over the leadership of the congregation. The congregation elected David Boese to be the leading minister. David Heidebrecht, however, continued to be the elder of the congregation.

Around this time the congregation also decided to add twenty feet to the church. I was appointed to be the foreman for the work. Johan Schmidt, Peter Dyck and Johan Baergen were elected to the building committee. Many of the congregation, or almost all, came and helped so that the building of the addition went quite well. We now had more space for Sunday School as well as space for a kitchen, and in the front of the basement there was room to hang our coats in winter. After four or five years the wooden floor was taken out of the basement, the basement was dug a foot deeper, and a cement floor made. Peter Neufeld, John Thiessen and Johnny Heidebrecht were now on the building committee and I was again the foreman. The soil had to be wheeled out with wheelbarrows. That was hard work but again quite a few had come to help. Then when Mom once came in the afternoon with a large pot of coffee with sandwiches for everyone, they all sat and had a coffee break. That was a good time back then when people could work together at the church. Later, people were hired for every little bit of work and paid. I must mention that the cement floor in the basement was made by a contractor from Edmonton.

Mrs. Driediger, who had been the janitor at the church for many years, left Tofield in 1958 and we took over the work of caretaker of the church. We did janitor work there for fifteen years until 1973 when we moved away from Tofield. At first, Mom and the children did the work. The last years, when the children were all gone from home, I helped Mom keep the church clean. For this work, we were paid. (See box below.)

Tofield Mennonite Church. Mrs. Driediger, the janitor and custodian of the church, lived in the house next to the church.

David Boese, who was the leading minister for 6½ years in the congregation, resigned from this position and, during a brotherhood council meeting (*Bruderberatung*) in 1955, I was elected as leading minister and Abe Baergen was elected as superintendent of the Sunday School in my place. This work, as leading minister of the congregation, was, for me, a great and difficult work. During the workday, I did carpentry work. Then often during the evening I visited sick people in the hospital. Mom helped me a lot. She

The monthly payment of $40.00 covered the cost of our grocery bill most months. I do not recall this "honorarium" being increased for the many hours spent cleaning the church every week during the years between 1958 and 1967. I was assigned much of that job before I left home in 1967. However, I discovered that "cleaning" was as much a ritual as a necessity, so I spent many hours playing the piano as a substitute for dusting the pews and hymn books plus a few other chores that I thought were unnecessary on a weekly basis.

often went along, particularly when women of the congregation were in the hospital. Then there were, otherwise, many times when I had to drive to people in the congregation when there were misunderstandings among brethren, but about this it is still too soon to write. (See box on p 154.) On Sunday for service, everything should also be ready. In the winter months there were the journeys for bible discussion to which I was commissioned by the Alberta Conference to participate. Of such a journey, I have written in detail in a little booklet. The congregation desired that I should also participate in the Alberta Conference. At brotherhood council meetings, I and several other brethren were elected to go to the conferences. In 1954, David Boese, George Franz and I were elected by the Alberta Conference to be on the Alberta Missions Committee. That term lasted until 1959. From 1956 to 1962, I and two other brethren from the Alberta Conference were elected for the Alberta Conference Program Committee.

Interior of the church. Men sat on the left, women on the right, the ministers to the left of the pulpit, and the choir to the right of the pulpit.

On occasion I suggested to Dad in jest that he wear a blue helmet to the church council meetings. I'm not sure that he realized that United Nations Peacekeepers wore blue helmets. (I also joked that the *Bruderberatung*, a "brotherhood council meeting," might have been more like a *Bruderbraten*, a "brother roast." Not very nice on my part, I admit.) There were also several times when couples that had conceived out of wedlock arrived at our house, embarrassed and fearful, to discuss how they might be married in a church that would severely censure their behaviour. Surprisingly, they usually left light-hearted and happy after speaking with Dad for some time. He always tried to bring people who had problems with other church members back into the fold with forgiveness and acceptance rather than censure and condemnation. How very admirable. I'm not surprised that he never did get around to writing later about the church's problems.

Elder D. Heidebrecht, whom I often asked for advice, died in 1957 during the last week in February and on March 1st was the funeral. On January 2, 1961, at a brotherhood council meeting, I resigned from the leadership of the congregation. David Regehr was then elected as the leading minister of the congregation. Now the congregation wanted to elect an elder again. On May 7, 1961, at a congregational meeting *(Gemeindestunde)* (now it was not a brotherhood meeting but a congregational meeting at which all the women could also vote) I was elected as Elder with more than two-thirds of the votes of the congregation. When David Regehr (the leading minister of the congregation) asked when our ordination as Elder could take place, we said, if the congregation agreed with it, we would wish it to be on August 6th. What a special day this has always been for us. On August 6, 1933, I was ordained as minister of the gospel. On August 6, 1939, Mom and I had our wedding and in August 1958 the congregation in Tofield celebrated 25 years of my having been a minister, and in 1964, on August 6, Mom and I celebrated our silver wedding in the Tofield church to which the whole congregation was invited.

In 1961, at the Canadian Mennonite Conference that was held in Calgary from July 5 – 11, I was elected to the Christian Service Board. I was on this board for four years. It was the last week in January in which the board meetings were always held at the Canadian Mennonite Bible College to which I went every year. Even if I was not able to help along much, I did gain a great insight into the college, the conference work, and particularly the Christian Service Board.

The congregation agreed that our ordination was to take place on August 6th. That again was a special day for us and also for the congregation. The elders C.G. Neufeld of Didsbury and Jacob D. Nickel of Rosemary performed the ordination. On this day, Abe Baergen and his wife were also ordained as ministers. Present on that day were the Tofield ministers, David Regehr, David Boese and Abe Heidebrecht; from Edmonton the ministers Art Dyck, Gerhardt Franz and Elder Herb Peters; from Didsbury, W. Pauls; from Calgary, Elder Otto Bartel and Elder Peter Heidebrecht and minister Peter Retzlaff who later became elder of the Coaldale congregation. Also, our siblings from B.C. and Rosemary had come. This work as Elder of the congregation again presented new tasks for me and Mom.

C.G. Neufeld, Abe Baergen, Katy Baergen, Louise Neufeld, John Neufeld, Jacob Nickel. The verse above the pulpit reads, HERR, ich habe lieb die Stätte deines Hauses und den Ort, da deine Ehre wohnet. LORD, I have loved the habitation of your house and the place where your glory dwells. Psalm 26:8.

Ministers in the Tofield Mennonite Church
Back row: George Franz, Abe Baergen, Frank Baergen (deacon), David Regehr.
Front row: David Boese, John Neufeld, Abe Heidebrecht, Abram Epp.

In the summer of 1956, I was in Winnipeg at the General Mennonite Conference where I was a delegate from the Tofield Mennonite Church.

In 1962 Mom and I went to Ontario. The Canadian Conference of Mennonites was held in St. Catharines. We stayed with our relatives, the Jake Rogalskis. Then, on August 2nd we were at the Mennonite World Conference in Kitchener, Ontario, for a day.

In 1966, from October 26th to November 2nd, I was at a minister's seminar in Elkhart, U.S.A., where ministers were given courses. On Sunday we were in Goshen in a church of the Old Mennonites next to Goshen College.

So, I was able to help, and I have gained some insight into the varied work of the Kingdom of God. In the local Mennonite Church in Tofield, I was able to help. Then I have been at the Alberta Mennonite Church Conference, at the Canadian Mennonite Conferences as well as once at the General Mennonite Conference, and once at the Mennonite World conference. At all these conferences at which I have been, I have been sent as a delegate by the Mennonite Church in Tofield except for the Mennonite World Conference in Kitchener.

Louise and John Neufeld (about 1961)

Descendants of John and Louise Neufeld

Dad did not write about his own children in 1977 when he penned his memoir. Since he was writing a family history for his children to read, he may have thought that we knew all the details of our marriages, our children, and where we lived and worked. So, understandably, he didn't include them in his memoir. Now, in the year 2022, John and Louise Neufeld would be very pleased to know that their children have been richly blessed with children and grandchildren of their own—John and Louise's great-grandchildren.

What follows are brief descriptions of the descendants of John and Louise Neufeld written in 2022 for future generations to read.

Linda Margaret Neufeld was a very successful elementary school teacher. Beginning in 1959, after one year of teacher education at the University of Alberta, as was common at that time, she taught elementary grades in Tofield from 1960 to 1962 and again from 1964 to 1965. She preferred to teach Grade 4 students, a time when children are often at their best. In between those years, Linda attended Canadian Mennonite Bible College (CMBC) in Winnipeg, the college that her future husbands Lorne Buhr and Hugo Peters also attended. She graduated in 1966. From 1966 to 1968 she taught school in Pauingassi, a remote, isolated First Nations community located about 280 kilometres northeast of Winnipeg. In the following years, she taught elementary school, one year in Calgary, and then she completed her career as a teacher in Okotoks in 1980.

From 1977 to 1979, and again from 1980 to 1982, Linda studied at the Associated Mennonite Biblical Seminaries (now Anabaptist Biblical Seminary) in Elkhart, Indiana. While on a work/study program in a hospital, she discovered her calling to chaplaincy. She then completed another year of training in hospital chaplaincy in South Bend, Indiana, after which she returned to Calgary where she continued further training in chaplaincy.

Ideally suited for the spiritual care and compassion required of a hospital chaplain, Linda served in the Charles Camsell, Royal Alexandra and Misericordia Hospitals in Edmonton from 1983 until her retirement in 2005. During that time Cleo, a stray cat, came to live with Linda. As a smart, funny, and delightful cat, she was a wonderful companion to Linda for three years.

Linda was ordained to ministry at Foothills Mennonite Church in Calgary on November 6, 1983. In addition to the very special work of a hospital chaplain ministering to sick and dying patients, their families and hospital staff, and conducting funeral services, she also faithfully served her church communities in Calgary and Edmonton for many years.

On July 21, 2001, Linda married **Lorne Buhr** whose first wife, Katherine (Linda's good friend), had died two years previously. Lorne was a retired librarian from the Legislature Library in the Legislative Assembly of Alberta. Linda and Lorne were deacons at First Mennonite Church in Edmonton with Linda presenting an occasional sermon. Lorne died on October 2, 2016, after a lengthy struggle with Parkinson's disease. Lorne and Linda were married for 15 years.

Linda is a much-loved stepmother to Lorne's three children, Patrick, Andrew, and Michael. **Patrick** is a library technician with Justice Canada. His wife, Evelyn, is the administrator at First Mennonite Church in Edmonton. They have two children: Thomas has a passion for music and plays the piano, and Natalie has just graduated from high school and is studying design. **Andrew** teaches high school upgrading in mathematics at Grant McEwan University in Edmonton and loves to play the Indian sitar. His wife's name is Cari. **Michael** teaches high school upgrading in physics and chemistry at Grant McEwan University.

After Lorne's death, Linda and **Hugo Peters** renewed a friendship that began when they were both students at the Canadian Mennonite Bible College in Winnipeg from which they both graduated. (Hugo's wife, Herta, died during the same month as Lorne's death.) That friendship blossomed over a couple of years leading to a happy marriage on July 28, 2018. Hugo was a high school Social Studies teacher for 31 years with a special interest in geography and world religions. Linda has now been blessed with another family of stepchildren, this time from Hugo's marriage to Herta. Hugo and Linda live in Winnipeg where, in retirement, they are both active members of Bethel Mennonite Church.

Hugo & Linda (2021)

Myrna Dyck, Hugo's first daughter, is an epidemiologist and is married to Darryl Dyck who works as a consultant for sales and servicing of medical imaging technology. They have three sons: **Matthew** (married to Autumn Rempel whose last name he took) graduated from Canadian Mennonite University and works in information technology and business plan development in the not-for-profit sector; **Ryan** has studied web design and is presently at Red River College Polytechnic studying computer programming; and **Brandon** who will graduate from the University of Manitoba as a mechanical engineer in 2022.

Renee Strempler, Hugo's second daughter, is a social worker with Child and Family Services, Manitoba. She is married to Rudy Strempler who is a sales representative with Belterra, a producer of industrial belts for mines and agriculture, etc. They have two sons. **Jordan** will graduate with degrees in Education and Kinesiology in 2022. **Jonathan** has studied carpentry at Red River College Polytechnic and presently works in construction. He is planning to study and train as a firefighter/paramedic.

Linda & Hugo with Hugo's children and grandchildren
Standing, L to R: Brandon Dyck, Autumn Rempel, Matthew (Dyck) Rempel,
Darryl Dyck, Myrna (Peters) Dyck, Hugo, Linda, Rudolf Strempler, Renee (Peters)
Strempler, Jordan Strempler. Kneeling: Ryan Dyck, Jonathan Strempler (2018)

Arnold John Neufeld loved reading books when he wasn't working hard at a job. As a youth, he already had a deep-seated sense of responsibility. When we still heated our little house in Tofield with wood and coal, you could find Arnold reading a book beside the stove long after midnight while he fed the fire with wood and coal during a howling winter blizzard at minus 30 degrees Fahrenheit. During the summer months, at ages 14 and 15, he was already working long hours with our neighbour, David Duguid, doing stucco and plaster work in the new houses being built in Tofield and area. Then at ages 16 and 17 he worked with Dad building houses for Charlie Kallal. After long workdays Arnold often enjoyed the social activities of an active church youth group.

After graduating from high school, Arnold attended Menno Bible Institute in Didsbury, Alberta. He then earned a Bachelor of Education with a major in Industrial Arts from the University of Calgary. After one year teaching industrial arts in Sexsmith, Alberta, he returned to Calgary where he took up employment in Kurt and Alfred Janz's Tower Construction company building many houses from 1967 to 1986. During this time he became a valued employee in the Janz brothers' company as the Production Manager where he was responsible for the many work crew leaders in his supervisory capacity. Arnold also studied carpentry at the Southern Alberta Institute for Technology where he won an award with top marks in Alberta in the fourth-year curriculum of the Carpenter Certification program. Following his work with *Tower Construction*, he took on several business ventures with friends and partners.

Arnold also had a passion for "church building," both literally and figuratively. Having helped to build new churches, together with his wife Marjorie he dedicated much of his time to creating church communities. Their warm hospitality and concern for young adults made an important contribution to each of the congregations where they served. Now, in addition to preparing meals two days each week for the kitchen at Centre Street Church in Calgary together with Marj, Arnold is still employed in a part-time job in his "retirement."

Arnold and **Marjorie** Anne Hildebrand met while serving at Camp Valaqua in the mid 1960s. They were married on July 2, 1966. Marjorie studied at the Calgary General Hospital where she worked as a Registered Nurse for several years. In 1973 Marjorie underwent major brain surgery (pituitary gland) that left her unemployable for many years. Then when their sons Jonathan and Lincoln were in junior high school, she began part-time work. Her first full-time job was working in a medical office for a general practitioner in Calgary and then for an internist. From there she worked on the North Hill for an endocrinologist and later was employed closer to their home as a receptionist for two family doctors. When they closed their practices, she became the booking clerk in a busy walk-in clinic. Before retiring in 2019, Marjorie's working life came to a fitting end as a receptionist for a gastroenterologist.

Since her retirement, she has been active volunteering at their church, having coffee with neighbours, and cooking many meals for family and friends.

Arnold & Marjorie Neufeld (2021)

Arnold and Marjorie were blessed with two sons, Jonathan Earl born November 6, 1969, and Lincoln James born May 7, 1971.

Jonathan attended school at the Heritage Christian Academy in Calgary. After graduating from the University of Calgary with a Bachelor of Education degree in 1991, he taught high school for three years in Three Hills, Alberta. Then he studied at Regent College in Vancouver, B.C., graduating with a Master of Divinity degree in 2003. Jonathan was assistant pastor at Wellingdon Church in Burnaby, B.C., for many years before his current position as lead pastor at Ridge Church in Maple Ridge, B.C.

Jonathan and **Noula** Chondronikolis were married on December 29, 2001. Noula is an elementary school teacher. Jonathan and Noula have three children. **Julia** Grace was born on March 21, 2003. Having recently graduated from high school, she is attending Qwanoes Bible School on Vancouver Island and serves as a lifeguard for the Qwanoes summer camp. **Zachary** John, born August 18, 2006, is currently in Grade 10 in Maple Ridge Secondary School.

An avid sports enthusiast, he enjoys mountain biking, hiking, and parkour games. **Sarah** Elise, born April 15, 2008, loves animals, horseback riding, baking fancy cakes and school. She is currently in Grade 8.

Sarah, Noula, Zachary, Jonathan, Julia Neufeld (2021)

Lincoln graduated from Heritage Christian Academy and then attended Columbia Bible College in Clearbrook, B.C. After that he worked as a carpenter framing houses with his uncle Dan for some years. Now he owns Roxolid Contracting Inc., an excavating company. He enjoys creating beautiful retaining walls with huge rocks in addition to general excavating. Lincoln married **Miriam** Sofia Eleanor Turvy on August 9, 1997. Lincoln and Miriam had four children.

Elijah Thomas, born October 22, 1998, graduated from John Diefenbaker High School in Calgary. He currently works as a plumber's assistant. Elijah enjoys rock climbing. **Eden** Jane, born November 5, 2000, also graduated from John Diefenbaker High School. She has worked with horses at Camp Evergreen in Sundrie, Alberta, as well as assisting in the camp kitchen. Eden is currently attending Three Hills Bible School enrolled in a program for emergency medical services (EMS), a profession that she would like to pursue. **Ruben** James, born

October 4, 2002, also graduated recently from John Diefenbaker High School and is now working as an electrician's assistant. He aspires to become an airline pilot. **Leah** Anne, born January 23, 2005, is a student at JDHS in Grade 11. She is an avid student and loves working with animals and people.

Lincoln's marriage with Miriam ended in divorce in January 2015. In June 2018, **Holly** Noelle DeGama became Lincoln's partner. Born on May 9, 1978, she completed both Bachelor and Master of Arts degrees from the University of Calgary. She then went on to complete a Bachelor of Science degree in Nursing from the University of Calgary. Holly is a registered emergency room nurse (RN) in Calgary. She has two children. **Rose** Emily DeGama Blanchet, born July 14, 2004, is in Grade 12, currently attending Joane Cardinal-Schubert High School. She has a love of art and music. **Philip** Jerrold DeGama Blanchet, born February 1, 2008, is in Grade 8 at Nickle Middle School in Calgary. He is an avid motorcycle racer and often wins races with older participants.

Back row: Ruben & Elijah Neufeld, Holly DeGama, Lincoln Neufeld.
Front row: Leah & Eden Neufeld, Rose & Philip DeGama Blanchet (2021)

Daniel Jacob Neufeld was a very creative child gifted with an extraordinary talent in the visual arts. Whether painting landscapes, doing taxidermy, creating intricate woodwork designs, or building beautiful furniture, he has used his creativity to generously enrich the lives of his family and community. After Grade 11 he chose to make carpentry his career. Within a few years, he formed his own company, Danfeld Framing Ltd. During 50 years as a very successful builder, he has framed 860 houses from 1200 to 5000 square feet in Calgary. In his retirement, Dan has continued with other building projects such as constructing complex decks and fences and, in his spare time, he has again taken up painting beautiful pictures and constructing an amazing miniature village in his basement.

Jannette & Dan (2021)

Dan and **Jannette** Kathleen Thiessen, born on December 9, 1949, in St. Boniface, Manitoba, were married on June 29, 1968. In addition to a busy life as a mother and grandmother, Jannette was manager of the deli and bakery at the Co-op supermarket in Calgary for many years. She also spent much time and effort volunteering at Foothills Mennonite Church and the MCC store in Calgary. Dan and Jannette continue a vibrant family life that includes weekly gatherings with their daughter Lisa, her husband Darcy, and their grandchildren as well as enjoying their fellowship with friends from their church.

Dan and Jannette were blessed with two daughters. **Michelle** Denise, born May 16, 1971, was married to **Adam** Robinson on May 14, 1994. Michelle was trained as a social worker and worked with mentally challenged adults. She also had planned to help schizophrenic women. While Adam was studying at the Associated Mennonite Seminary in Elkhart, Indiana, Michelle and Adam came to Guelph, Ontario, for a visit. There she was hospitalized and then sent to McMaster Hospital in Hamilton where she struggled, midway through her first pregnancy, to recover from a rare condition called Ehlers-Danlos Syndrome. Sadly, after a brief recuperation period, Michelle died on April 26, 1999, of a pulmonary embolism when she also lost her daughter Claire. Michelle's death has been a great loss for her family and for us all as she was such a wonderful blessing to her family, her professional colleagues, and her church community. Adam, a minister, remains a much-loved member of Dan and Jannette's family. He is married to Karen Beckert with two children, Eric and Sophie.

Lisa, Adam, Michelle, Jannette, Dan (May 14, 1994)

Lisa Dawn, born November 21, 1973, has been a teaching assistant for special needs children for seventeen years while enriching the lives of her happy family of four children when they were still at home. On June 3, 1995 she is married to **Darcy** Garret Krahn, whom she met while a student at Columbia Bible College in Abbotsford, B.C. Darcy studied horticulture and landscaping for two years at Olds College in Alberta. In addition to landscaping during the warmer months, his company, Green Acres Landscaping, does snow removal and property management during the winter.

Lisa and Darcy Krahn (2021)

Lisa and Darcy have four children. **Kennedy** Paige, born June 3, 1997, is presently a nanny for two boys aged three and six months. She was employed for several years at The Manor in Calgary. Kennedy loves photography and hiking in her spare time. **Nathaniel** (Nate) Jacob, born November 29, 1999, was employed as a framer building houses for some years but now works at *Eight Ounce Coffee,* a company that specializes in exclusive coffee equipment for Canadian baristas and coffee drinkers. He was in Hawaii last year serving with Youth With a Mission when his work was interrupted by the COVID-19 pandemic. Nate enjoys working with children and has a very active interest in sports. **Samuel** (Sam) Garret, born June 23, 2002, is currently employed in sales at Sport Chek, a retail outlet for sports shoes and clothing. In the summer of 2021, Sam toured Paris, Rome, Genoa, Milan, and Barcelona where he indulged his passion for art at the many galleries he and his friend visited. **Charlie** Adam, born April 22, 2004, is in Grade 12 at Robert Thirsk High School. An avid sportsman, he excels in playing volleyball and basketball. Charlie has recently been accepted into the sports broadcasting program at the Southern Alberta Institute for Technology in Calgary. His extraordinary memory for sports statistics will be a major asset in his chosen profession.

As a close-knit family, Darcy, Lisa, and their children are "best friends" with family activities playing an important and enjoyable role in their lives.

Kennedy, Nate, Sam, and Charlie Krahn (2021)

Gerald Peter Neufeld enjoyed going to school, reading books, and playing the piano, guitar, and trumpet. He played first trumpet in the Edmonton Cosmopolitan Band while in high school, travelling to Edmonton with Bert Everitt, the local butcher/philosopher. With support from Linda, he agreed to attend the Canadian Mennonite Bible College (CMBC) in Winnipeg for a year so that he could study music before pursuing a "real" profession. There he realized his real passion was conducting choral music, and there he met **Elizabeth** (Betty, Betts) Violet Peters, a singer and fellow music student. They were married in 1970.

After three wonderful, life-changing years at CMBC, Gerald completed an undergraduate degree in music at the University of Manitoba. He and Elizabeth then spent four years studying music at the Nordwestdeutsche Musikakademie in Detmold, Germany. Elizabeth excelled as a singer while Gerald studied choral and orchestral conducting. A year after returning to Canada, they both taught at the University of Guelph for ten years. Gerald earned a Doctor of Musical Arts degree from the University of Iowa during a two-year leave of absence from the University of Guelph from 1983 – 1985. In 1991 he was hired as a full-time professor in the Music Faculty at the University of Western Ontario (London, Ontario) conducting choirs and teaching choral conducting until his retirement in 2016. However, his most rewarding work was with the Guelph Chamber Choir, which he conducted for 37 years from its founding in 1980 until 2019.

While conducting choirs and orchestras in more than 500 concerts in Canada and on several choir tours in Europe, Britain, and Canada, the boy who dreamed of conducting Handel's *Hallelujah Chorus* just once has had the good fortune to conduct Handel's *Messiah* in over 30 concerts. Making music together with wonderful singers and musicians has been his passion and a joy throughout his adult life.

Gerald and Elizabeth were blessed with two children: Jerome, born on August 26, 1978, and Nicole, born on August 7, 1981.

After Elizabeth spent some years on a quest for self discovery, she and Gerald found themselves on separate paths in life's journey, and in 1993 they separated. Sadly, Elizabeth died on January 19, 2022, after having suffered a massive aneurysm on Christmas Day. Wayne Bieman, her partner of 15 years, her children, grandchildren, and all of us mourn her passing.

Left: Nicole, Gerald, Jerome, Elizabeth Neufeld (1990)
Right: Patricia Eton-Neufeld (2002)

For several years after his separation, Gerald enjoyed the daily companionship of Jerome and Nicole. Gerald met **Patricia** (Pat) Eton in 1996 when she served on a Guelph Chamber Choir committee planning the choir's yearly fundraising cabaret. She and Gerald were married in 1998, and Pat has become a much-loved partner, stepmother, grandmother, and member of the extended family. In her youth, Pat loved sports and played on the Ontario Women's Field Hockey Team. She earned a Bachelor of Science degree in biology from the University of Guelph and, while being employed, earned another bachelor's degree in economics plus she competed further studies in accounting at Wilfrid Laurier University in Waterloo. Pat has worked as an administrator and accountant for non-profit organizations throughout her career and was the administrator for the Guelph Chamber Choir for 20 years. Her love of her grandchildren and affection for children in general has been a blessing for us, and she now enjoys volunteering in junior and senior kindergarten classes at King George Public School in Guelph.

Pat and Gerry (2021)

As a child **Jerome** Anthony Neufeld couldn't seem to fit enough activity into a twenty-four-hour day. He enjoyed the friends and challenges of school and, from the age of three, learned to play the violin in the Guelph Suzuki School. Along with many hours spent practicing violin music, he sang in school choirs and played oboe in the band at Oakridge High School in London, Ontario. Playing soccer from an early age was another of Jerome's many passions, and he was chosen to play on the London Representative Team, a soccer team that competed in tournaments in Canada, the USA, and twice in Italy.

Jerome began his post-secondary education at the University of Toronto where he earned a Bachelor of Applied Science in Engineering Science degree and a Master of Science degree in physics. Following completion of a PhD degree in geophysics at Yale University, he continued with post-doctoral work at Cambridge University in England where he now is Professor of Earth and Planetary Fluid Dynamics in both the Department of Earth Sciences and the Department of Applied Mathematics and Theoretical Physics. He is also a Fellow in Natural Sciences (mathematics) at Trinity College, Cambridge.

When not teaching and mentoring graduate students, Jerome's latest research seeks to understand the fluid dynamical behaviour of Earth and other planetary bodies. Carbon sequestration, an important means of capturing and storing carbon dioxide, is also among his various research projects.

Jerome and **Sharon** Ann Scovil were married on June 21, 2003. Sharon graduated with a Bachelor of Social Science degree in psychology from the University of Waterloo in Ontario. While there, she lived at Conrad Grebel College and sang in the Chapel Choir directed by Leonard Enns. Sharon was a researcher in obstetrics and gynecology at Yale University, developing HIV-AIDS interventions. As well as training researchers in South Africa, she worked on projects to ameliorate the spread of AIDS from mothers to children in that country. After several years as a researcher at Cambridge University, Sharon completed a PhD degree in Psychology from that university in 2019. Among her many research projects, she studies the effectiveness of community-based mental health services for adolescents and young adults in England.

Sharon has sung in early music choirs such as Arcady Ensemble in Brantford, Ontario, and the Yale Camerata. She sings in and has directed the church choir at St. Andrew's Church in Cambridge, and she enjoys playing ultimate frisbee and running long distances in her spare time.

Jerome and Sharon have three children: Cayley Rose, born December 12, 2007; Miles Ephraim, born September 24, 2010; and Wendell Isaac, born April 28, 2013.

Cayley is in Year 10 in Chesterton Community College in Cambridge where drama classes are her favourite activity. As well as reading lots of novels, Cayley enjoys music and swimming. She is training to be a lifeguard as well as coaching younger children in their swimming classes.

Miles is in year 7 in Chesterton Community College. An avid sportsman, Miles excels in football (soccer) and enjoys playing the piano and swimming. In Year 6, he was given the lead role in the final drama production, and, with his kind and generous nature, Miles helps his classmates whenever he can.

Wendell is in Year 5 in Milton Road Primary School. A budding naturalist, he enjoys birds, animals, and generally discovering the workings of the universe when not reading his siblings' novels. Wendell has a very affectionate personality and his amusing and whimsical nature is often on display.

Sharon, Jerome, Wendell, Cayley, and Miles Neufeld (2021)

As a child, **Nicole** Elizabeth Neufeld played cello for 16 years. However, she also enjoyed drawing, painting, sewing, crafts, dance, and creating artistic items. It was art classes that she really enjoyed in high school, and in London she attended H. B. Beal Secondary School where she immersed herself in a program specializing in visual arts. While initially studying architecture at the University of Toronto, Nicole realized that art history was her dominant interest and so she completed a Bachelor of Arts degree majoring in art history at the University of Guelph.

After completing a Master of Arts degree with distinction in art history from Carleton University in Ottawa, Nicole was employed by the Museum of Contemporary Canadian Art in Toronto and the Kitchener-Waterloo Art Gallery where she was Director of Public Programming. Then, following three years employed by the River Run Centre in Guelph as Program Manager, Development and Marketing, she now serves as the Community Engagement Coordinator in the Art Gallery of Guelph.

Nicole met **Michael** Roman Hryn at a blues festival in Ottawa in 2007. They were married on Mike's family's farm on August 24, 2013. Mike grew up on a hobby farm north of Guelph where his stepfather, Bill Mactaggart, raised prize-winning show sheep. Mike worked on the farm and briefly in an abattoir during his high school years. After studying marketing and communications at Mohawk College in Hamilton, he was employed in sales for Molson for a couple of years. In September 2008, a week after the market crash, Mike joined the Mactaggart family business in Guelph with his stepbrother, Will, where he now is a successful portfolio and investment advisor. Mike and Will are very involved in the Guelph community in numerous ways such as the Oak Tree Project's funding for support this year of people experiencing homelessness.

Nicole and Mike enjoy attending concerts, hiking, traveling, and (of course) visiting art galleries in many cities. They have two sons: Holden was born on February 8, 2015, and Clint was born on July 1, 2017, Canada's 150th anniversary.

With his vivid imagination and lots of Lego, **Holden** Michael Hryn enjoys building all kinds of creative structures. Now in a Grade 2 French Immersion class in King George Public School, he excels at all things with numbers, and he is already a competent chess player who enjoys winning games playing against Grandma Pat. Playing hockey and running games are a lot of fun for Holden as well as playing with his brother Clint.

Clinton John Hryn is in the Senior Kindergarten French Immersion class in King George Public School where he enjoys a variety of activities with his classmates. Clint indulges his creativity in all things artistic like drawing and colouring pictures as well as various other interesting crafts. He enjoys cooking and baking, generally helping around with house and outdoor work, and wrestling with Holden.

Nearby St. George's Park presents lots of opportunities for both boys to test the limits of their climbing ability with other kids in the neighbourhood on a very high playground structure. Splashing in Grandma Leslie Mactaggart's swimming pool at the farm during hot summer months and playing hockey on the ice rink in the sheep barn during winter months provide hours of fun and physical activity for both Clint and Holden.

Nicole Neufeld, Clint, Holden, and Mike Hryn

A Family History
written by Patricia Eton-Neufeld

War and revolution are terrible events in themselves and they destroy so many families. They also result in political and religious refugees having no choice but to flee for their lives, leaving their villages and countries, sometimes not knowing where their final destination might be. World War II was a pivotal event for my parents, an event that resulted in Gerry and me meeting many years later and, happily, becoming the fortunate grandparents to Cayley, Miles, Wendell, Holden, and Clint.

My mother, Sheila Kilpatrick, born on September 4, 1929, in Liverpool, England, turned 10 the day after Great Britain and France declared war on Germany in 1939. My dad, Arpad Esztelecky, was born in Szeged, Hungary, on October 17, 1923, and so he was on the cusp of turning 16 in September 1939. The declaration of war resulted in their childhood and high school years being unimaginably changed. Those who lived through World War II did not often talk about their experiences. But I do remember my two brothers and me asking them to tell us war stories, usually in the middle of a thunderstorm or a snowstorm when the electricity was out. We would sit together in the light of a candle with the wind and rain lashing our windows or the snow piling high on the yard where we lived on a farm near Arthur, Ontario.

My parents met in England after the war while Dad was boarding at my mother's Aunt Kitty's house in Blackpool. Housing was in such short supply after the war that people had to open their homes to boarders.

Mom and Dad were married on March 15, 1951, in Liverpool and came to Canada on the SS Homeland, landing in Halifax on February 16, 1952. Many people emigrated from England during this time as many, still living on rations in a country decimated by war, struggled to recover. Ships left weekly from Liverpool—one week to Canada and one week to Australia. It sounded like their opportunity to become Australians was as great as their chance of being Canadians. What was the reason for leaving England? My father was a Catholic and my mother was a Church of England Protestant. At that time, animosity between those two groups was still very high, and the kindest thing one could say about Dad's spoken English was that it was "broken English."

My dad arrived in England after fleeing from Hungary after the war with no identification papers and with just the clothes on his back. He literally walked across the Hungarian border into Austria while on a lunch break with Hungarian workers. Why he felt compelled to leave Hungary is not clear, but he had been warned that the Communist authorities were looking for him at that time. Dad eventually arrived in Liverpool via Marseilles and Cambridge where he received instruction in English. In England and Scotland, he found employment with companies boring tunnels. He was well compensated even though he was a foreigner "without an identity." Then Britain issued him a travel document that allowed him to enter Canada in 1951 as an international refugee.

During this time of turmoil in Europe, fleeing one's country without documentation was not unusual. These refugees were known as DPs— Displaced Persons. In a class society, as England still was at that time, my parents' marriage would always be problematic as my mom, who had attended a high school for girls on a scholarship, was considered in a different class from my dad. My parents thought that with hard work they could build a new life for themselves in a country far away from the ravages of war and free of "old world" prejudices.

And so they set about getting jobs in Canada and in time they bought a house and a car. Dad was granted Canadian citizenship in July 1957—the year I was born on December 6th. Michael followed on May 8, 1959, and Peter on March 5, 1964.

Mom's death from cancer on April 2, 1987, certainly changed the trajectory of my life and made me think about the meaning of life and what contribution I was going to make to society. In July 1993, Dad married his brother Joe's widow, Angi, in Stratford, Ontario, and returned to Hungary to live in Szeged where they both grew up. After the fall of Communism in 1989, the Hungarian government gave Dad back his Hungarian passport. He happily lived out his senior years with Angi in Szeged, the city where he was born, providing much needed assistance to his extended family during the years of transition following the fall of Communism. On October 23, 2021, he died in

Szeged at the age of 98. Angi died shortly after on April 15, 2022, at the age of 87.

Details of Gerry's and my parents' histories differ but the themes are very similar. They were principled people of courage who overcame the ravages of war and gave up everything to begin life in a new country. We are very fortunate to have been born in this country and, although Gerry and I may have very different skills and professions, we share so very many values as well as the outlook on life that our parents bequeathed us. Although our parents came from different countries, they all valued kindness, generosity, respect for others, a natural inclination to hard work, commitment to the people in their communities and, most of all, a commitment and love for every member of their extended families regardless of birth or origin of country.

As of this writing Gerry and I have been double vaccinated for the COVID-19 virus as the world-wide pandemic is in the fourth surge of the virus. Over two years of lockdown during the pandemic have offered us time to contemplate how people meet each other and how families are formed that would normally not have happened were it not for the great wars and revolutions of a previous century. Our stories have been interwoven within the tapestry of a Canadian history that has been very kind to the dispossessed of the world. It is because of our parents' and grandparents' decisions to seek a better life in a "new world" that we now enjoy a wonderful life in a peaceful, multinational country. For this we are truly grateful.

Afterword

As I write these words in the summer of 2022, forty-five years after Dad wrote his memoir, our thoughts are with the Ukrainian people who are valiantly trying to defend themselves against the invasion of their country by the Russian army. Russian President Vladimir Putin, a leader who has taken complete control of the Russian "electoral" system as well as the state media and most of the functions of government, has been able to manipulate state institutions of power and much of the Russian population to his will through mass propaganda measures. The invasion of Ukraine is based on Putin's false pretext that it is a "military action" to suppress a Nazi movement in Ukraine and his desire to "liberate" the Ukrainian people. With the help of NATO countries and the very strong resistance of the Ukrainian people, Russia has *not* been able, to date, to subject the Ukrainian people to its will and enfold the Ukrainian nation back into the Russian Federation.

Much of this war seems to reflect a time 100 years ago under the dictatorship of Joseph Stalin. The Russian army has been mandated to terrorize the civilian population in eastern Ukraine. Mariupol, a city about 100 kilometres east of where the villages of Marienthal and Pordenau were once located, has been almost entirely destroyed during three months of relentless bombardment of industrial and residential buildings and structures. Thousands of civilians have perished in the unrelenting onslaught of Russia's military forces. Unfortunately, tens of thousands of Russian military personnel have also died in this senseless aggression against a peaceful country that shares a 2000-kilometre border with Russia. Many of the young Russians serving in the military do not know why they were ordered to invade Ukraine and have no desire to be there. Much like the Stalinist period following the Russian Revolution, the lives of millions of people in both Ukraine and Russia have been permanently altered and thousands have died because of the whims and wishes of a leader who makes decisions while living in isolation from the lived reality of the people under his rule.

About six million people have fled Ukraine already this year with another eight million being displaced in their own country. Is this a replication of the terror that motivated thousands of Mennonites to emigrate to Canada and the United States in the 1920s? What were the circumstances and considerations that convinced the families of our parents to leave comfortable, prosperous villages in Russia/Ukraine for new beginnings in a foreign country with a foreign language? It was the realization that all could be taken from them by the Communist system. It was a need to live in a country where they could live out their religious convictions without fear of military or government intervention—a country where they were exempt from military service.

It is difficult to imagine the soul-searching that must have accompanied the decision to leave all they had in Russia and begin a new life in a foreign land with a challenging climate. A deep abiding faith in a benevolent God was our parents' sure anchor in the stormy seas of dislocation and immigration.

Dad's entire life was one of deep faith in a compassionate God who would guide them through their most difficult experiences to lead a kinder, more compassionate and understanding life. Yet he spoke very little about his faith with his children. He just lived it with as much integrity as he could in every situation. I recall with much tenderness how, during a difficult time in my life, I was able to spend an hour with Dad at his hospital bed the night before he died. It was just two weeks after the marital separation between Elizabeth and me. At the end of a gentle conversation with Dad, punctuated by intervals of deep silence, he said, "You will be fine. Everything will be as it should." It was another example of Dad's faith that our wellbeing would be secure if we lived by the teachings and principles of a loving God. His assurance on his deathbed has been born out in the many good people and wonderful experiences I have had since his death in 1993.

I recall, while waiting for the church service to begin celebrating Mom and Dad's 50th wedding anniversary, that I said to Dan in jest, "I think Dad spent 20 minutes with me as a kid. It was the third day of a blizzard and he wanted to play checkers with me." With a twinkle in his eye, Dan gave his usual clever response, "So, how do you rank as favoured son?" That brought a good laugh from the three of us sons. Yes, his children may have wished for more parental engagement, but I am reminded again while reading his memoir that immigrant parents seldom had "kid time" in their daily schedule. And certainly, for those immigrants with two full-time jobs (as Dad had with carpentry and church work), there really wasn't time for "play." That simply wasn't done 70 years ago.

While reading Dad's memoir, I realized that he had already parented his siblings, especially his half-siblings. He had endured the loss of parents and homeland, he had created a new life in a new country with his brothers and sisters, and he had provided for a family of six throughout his later adult life. It is surprising that "number four child" enjoyed even 20 minutes of play time. Yet we imbibe the principles and habits our parents taught us and we seek to live according to them in our daily work and life.

We may have devoted much more time to our children than our parents did, but we each gave much to the church in our own way, too; Linda as an ordained pastor and hospital chaplain, Arnold as a builder of churches both physically and communally, Dan as a highly valued contributor to the physical and social functioning of a church, and Gerald as he conducted hundreds of concerts with sacred choral music in churches throughout Canada and Europe.

"The apple falls not far from the tree."

For copies of *What I Have Seen, Heard and Experienced* by John Neufeld in both English and German, contact Gerald Neufeld at <gneufeld@uwo.ca>. A photocopy of John Neufeld's original hand-written copy is also available.

Appendix 1: Anabaptists as Revolutionaries
by Cornelius J. Dyck

In turning to the sixteenth century we are struck by the extremely harsh names with which the Anabaptists were identified by some of their contemporaries who honestly considered them to be tools of the devil. For the most part, however, these were persons in authority in Catholic or Protestant churches, or in the state. The common people were not unfriendly to the Anabaptists unless they were aroused by the authorities. The hatred of officials was, in fact, poured out upon the Anabaptists precisely because they were so popular with the people.

When we search for the reasons for this popularity, we soon discover that the clean living and simple faith of the Anabaptists met a deep longing in the hearts of the people who were disgusted with the corruption of the church and the oppression of the state. In redefining the nature of the church to consist of believers only, the Anabaptists were also redefining the nature of the state since church and state were one society which all were expected to enter through infant baptism. As heretics they were thus also considered to be revolutionaries, people intent on undermining the state. The charge of sedition, of revolution, is very common in the records of the court hearings available to us.

There were other reasons for this charge in addition to their rejection of infant baptism as the rite of passage into the church. They refused to swear an oath of any kind, including the required annual oath of loyalty to the state; they would not serve as soldiers and most believed a Christian should not be in government; because of persecution they frequently met at unusual times and places, giving the further impression of secrecy and subversion. Besides this, they were extremely zealous promoters of their cause, ignoring all risks for the sake of spreading their faith. Felix Mantz was one of the first of many who died because they would not promise to keep quiet about their faith. When they were caught and tortured and burned, they died as victors, not as victims of a cruel age, confident to the end that their cause would ultimately triumph. All of these signs convinced the authorities that they were dealing with dangerous revolutionaries for whom the only answer was death.

There was a final major reason for calling the Anabaptists revolutionaries. Revolution meant violence to the authorities. The tragic events of the Peasants' Revolt under the leadership of Thomas Müntzer convinced them that all Anabaptists were revolutionary at heart. Even the most peaceful, they said, were no more than wolves in sheep's clothing waiting for the right moment to overthrow all government and order: "For although Müntzer is thrown down yet his spirit is not; it lives even yet, indeed rules in many corners—especially in the Anabaptist sect which was planted by Müntzer in this part of the land— and it has been impossible up to now to root it out."

Cornelius J. Dyck, An Introduction to Mennonite History, 3rd ed. (Waterloo, Ontario: Herald Press, 1993), 431- 432.

Appendix 2: Barbara (Funk) Neufeld's Family

Now something about Mother's family. Mother's father died in 1914 and her mother died in 1917. Mother had two brothers and two sisters. Heinrich, her oldest brother who was __ years younger than Mother, married Anna Thiessen from the village of Paulsheim. They also emigrated to Canada in 1926. They lived in Saskatchewan at Colonsay for six months. Then they moved to Beaverlodge, Alberta, where we then lived. Then they moved onto a homestead in Lynburn. They were very poor but enjoyed it here. He loved to clear the land and plough it, seeding, and harvesting. In the 1950s, I am not sure which year, they moved to Ontario. Soon after, he died. His wife now lives in a senior citizens' home in Vineland Ontario. They had six children. Agnes married a non-Mennonite man. Mrs. Funk once said that Agnes is not very happy. Henry married a Birby girl and lives on his father's farm. George married Marj Hoepner and they live near Tofield. John and Pete are both married and live in St. Catharines, Ontario. Louise's husband is Abe Dick—they live in Vineland, Ontario.

Mother's other brother, Gerhard, never married. Owing to circumstances, he did not emigrate to Canada. Instead, he went, via East Russia near the Amur River, to China. Then he went to Argentina, South America, where he lived alone, and he also died there.

Mother's sisters, Aganeta and Liese, married on the same day. Aganeta married Hans Dick who was a teacher. Their marriage was an unhappy one. She died after two years, and her little boy died as well.

(See photo on page 76 for the Funk family at their father Gerhard's funeral.)

Appendix 3: Immigration Documents

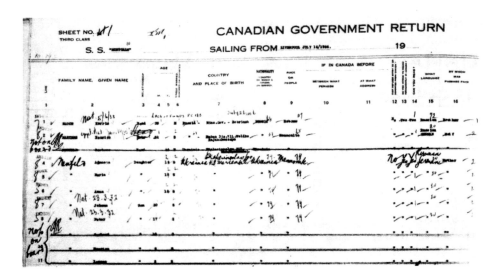

Part 1: Sheet No. 41 of *Canadian Government Return, Canadian Immigration Service* in the archives of the *Canadian Museum of Immigration at Pier 21* in Halifax. Subheading: *Sailing from Liverpool* 16 July 1926.

Lines 3 to 11 include the names of all nine members of the Neufeld family. However, lines 3, 9, 10, and 11 are crossed out with a handwritten note, "not on board." The names are Barbara (3), Gerhard (9), Heinrich (10), and Isaac (11). Obviously, they had originally been booked to travel on the same ship, the Montcalm.

The names of the five Neufeld siblings listed in lines 4 to 8 are as follows: Neufeld Aganeta (Agnes), Maria, Anna, Johann, Peter. Column 3 states whether they are daughters or sons. Columns 4 and 5 state their age. Column 4 shows Johann's age to be 20 and Peter to be 17. Column 5 shows Aganeta as 12, Maria as 19, and Anna as 15. Column 6, SINGLE, MARRIED, WIDOWED OR DIVORCED, identifies them all 5 siblings as single.

On the 4th line, the handwritten information under column 7, COUNTRY AND PLACE OF BIRTH reads *Ekaterinoslav for Ukrainia til (?) Mariental.*

(Ekaterinoslav is present-day Dnepro on the Dnieper River north of the Moloschna region.) Under Column 8, COUNTRY OF WHICH A CITIZEN OR RESIDENCY is *Ukrainia*. Column 9, RACE OR PEOPLE states *Mennonite*. Questions in columns 12, 13, and 14 with the written responses include (12) EVER REFUSED ENTRY TO OR EXPORTED FROM CANADA, *No*, (13) DO YOU INTEND TO RESIDE PERMANENTLY IN CANADA, *Yes*, (14) CAN YOU READ, *Yes*, *Russian, German*.

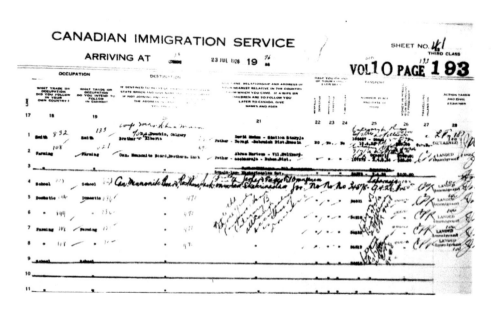

Part 2: Sheet No. 41 of *Canadian Government Return, Canadian Immigration Service* in the archives of the *Canadian Museum of Immigration at Pier 21* in Halifax. Subheading: *Arriving at Quebec* 23 July 1926.

Questions in the first two columns, 18 and 19, ask WHAT TRADE OR OCCUPATION DID YOU FOLLOW IN YOUR OWN COUNTRY and WHAT TRADE OR OCCUPATION DO YOU INTEND TO FOLLOW IN CANADA. Aganetha (Agnes) is listed as *school*, Maria and Anna as *domestic*, and Johann and Peter as *farming*. Column 20 notes who or what organization is sponsoring them: *Canadian Mennonite Board, Rosthern, Sask.* (The second passenger, Heinrich

Martens, is also sponsored by the Canadian Mennonite Board in Rosthern, Saskatchewan.) In Column 21 Gerhard (?) is listed as the brother-in-law of Barbara Neufeld. Underneath that a handwritten note reads, *"note the three girls' passports have Category B all carrying occupations as that of Domestic."* (Might Category B have referred to children or people without an occupation?) Columns 22, 23 and 24 note that none of the family had physical or mental defects.

Column 25, NUMBER, PLACE, AND DATE OF ISSUE, shows the passports as having been issued in Saporasja (present-day Zaporizhzhia) on April 9, 1926, although Dad's memoir says that Mr. Wichert received them in Karkow (Kharkiv). A handwritten note states, *Category B, Riga 7/7/26. a o Rosthern (?, difficult to read) CPR 9408*. Column 26, MONEY IN POSSESSION BELONGING TO PASSENGER shows a total of $150.00 for them all. Column 27, TRAVELLING INLAND ON lists *CPR* (Canadian Pacific Railway) and Column 28 titled ACTION TAKEN shows everyone as *Landed Immigrant*, followed (presumably) by the initials of the immigration officer.

Canadian Mennonite Board of Colonization
First members of Dad's Neufeld family to arrive in Canada.

Translation of above *Canadian Mennonite Board of Colonization* form.

	Family directory			Traveled on contract of not. _no_	
	List number	First, father's and family name	When born	Where born
Wife, Louise Enns	M178	Johann, Johann, Neufeld	6, June. 1905	Marienthal
Wife (of) Jacob J. Thiessen	L260	-------- " -------- Maria	28, Oct. 1906	----------
Wife Cornelia (Klassen)	N71	--------- " -------- Peter	19 Aug. 1908	----------
Wife (of) Jacob Joh. Rogalski	H364	--------- " -------- Anna	23 Oct. 1910	----------
Wife (of) John J. Thiessen	J27	--------- " -------- Aganetha (Agnes)	23 Nov. 1913	----------

Jahrgang (year's issue)   S (Seite = page?)   C (?)

189

Canadian Mennonite Board of Colonization
Second group of Neufeld family to arrive in Canada.

Translation of above *Canadian Mennonite Board of Colonization* form:
Last place of residence in Russia Marienthal
Departed from Nelgowka, Russia, on 15 June 1926, in Rezekne
Latvia arrived on 5 July, from Rezekne departed on July 9,
(Riga is handwritten over the word "Latvia.")
arrived in Libau on _____, departed from Libau on _____,
steamship Balluger.
In London, England, arrived on 13 July, from Liverpool,
departed on 16 July, steamship Montcalm.
In Quebec, Canada, landed on 23 July 1926.
First stay in Canada. Rosthern
Relatives in Canada or United States _____
List of members of this family who stayed behind on their way.

List number	First, father's and family name	When born	Where left behind	Why left behind
Widow(?)	Neufeld, Barbara	16 Dec. 1882	Southampton	with children because of ulcers (scabies)
	--- " ---, Gerhard (George)	23 Nov. 1916		
	--- ' ---, Heinrich (Henry)	21 Nov. 1917		
	--- " --- Isaac	31 May. 1921		

190

Part 5: *Canadian Mennonite Board of Colonization*
Members of Mom's Enns family to arrive in Canada.

Translation:

		Family directory	Traveled on contract of not. <u>no</u>	
	List number	First, father's and family name	When born	Where born
		Enns Jacob Nic. 56	8 Aug. 1870	
died 20.10.??		-- " – Margaretha 52	3 Dec. 1873	
wife (to) C. J. Fast	M309	-- " – Margaretha	21 Dec. 1905	
wife Anna (Kaethler)	H362	-- " – Peter	20 Nov. 1907	
wife (to) Joh. Jac. Thiessen	L266	-- " – Susanna	25 Nov. 1909	
wife Frieda Braul	H363	-- " – Nicolai	12 Jan. 1913	
wife (to) Joh. Joh. Neufeld	L116	-- " – Elisabeth	1 Mar. 1916	

Jahrgang (year's issue)   S (Seite = page?)   C (?)

Part 6: *Canadian Mennonite Board of Colonization*
(Were Mom's parents detained in Winnipeg?)

Translation:

Last place of residence in Russia Pordenau

Departed from Nelgowka, Russia, on 30 Sept 1926, in Rezekne

Latvia, arrived on 6 Oct, from Rezekne departed on 7 Oct.

(Rezekne has been replaced twice with handwritten Riga)

arrived in Libau on ___, departed from Libau on ____,

steamship Balluger

In London, England, arrived on Oct 19, from Southampton,

departed on Oct 21st, steamship Melita.

In Quebec, Canada, landed on Oct 29th, 1926.

First stay in Canada. Rosthern Sask

Relatives in Canada or United States c/o Jac. Enns – Eigenheimer Church

List of members of this family who stayed behind on their way.

List no.	First, father's and family name	When born	Where left behind	Why left behind
	Enns Jacob	56	Quebec	Arrived Winnipeg Nov. 4th 1926
	Margaretha	52		

Appendix 4: Siblings of Jacob Enns (Louise's father)

Father's sister, Sarah, was born on February 13, 1873, in the village of Gnadenheim. In 1896 she married Jacob Klassen of Eliesabetthal where her parents had moved. She was Jacob Klassen's second wife, the first one having died. The Lord granted them six children. Katharina married Aaron Wiebe. Sara Married Jacob Friesen and Jacob married Lena Funk. These three were married in Russia. Then in 1926 the whole family emigrated to Canada. In 1927 they moved to Beaverlodge. Here my brother Peter married Nellie on June 26, 1931, and Justina married Abram Wiens. In 1939 the whole Klassen family moved to Tofield. John married Maria Isaac. In 1944 Mr. Klassen died in Tofield and in 1947 the Abram Wienses, and Mrs. Klassen with them, moved to Ontario. Only the Peter Neufelds stayed in Tofield. Mrs. Klassen died on February 5, 1962. When they lived near Beaverlodge, we stayed at their place quite often when we travelled from Rio Grande to Beaverlodge. Jacob Friesen and his wife both died in Vineland, Ontario, also Jacob Klassen and his wife. John Klassen died in Yarrow, B.C.

Father's second sister was Katharina. She was born on March 20, 1875, in the village of Gnadenheim. In 1900 she married Henry Peters. The wedding was in the village of Eliesabetthal where her parents lived. Henry Peters was probably from the village of Gnadenheim. He was a widower left with three children from the first marriage. Two of these children died when they were small, and the other daughter died after she was already married. The Lord granted Henry and his wife eight children. John married Sara Neufeld, Henry married Maria Plet who died, and then he married Mrs. Herman Tessman who was a widow. Her maiden name was Anna Balzer. Jacob died when he was 15 years old in 1919 during the time that he and I were attending the high school (*Fortbildungsschule*) in Alexandertal. Katharina married Jacob Funk, Sara married Johan Nickel, Maria married Henry Braul, Nickolai married Liese (Louise) Klassen, and Abram married ??. All the spouses were from the village of Marienthal. I'm not sure where the Henry Peters lived at first, however, in 1914 they bought the Johan Schmidts' farm. It was a very fine farm. In 1926, when many from our village emigrated (among whom we were as well as Mrs. Peters' siblings, the Ennses and Klassens), then he did not want to emigrate. But in 1928 he wrote to the Ennses many times asking that they help him get his large family out. It was, however, then already impossible to emigrate because Russia had closed the door to emigration. Already before the Second World War most of the men of the Peters family were deported and the women evacuated to Germany by the Germans. Some of these were sent back (to Russia) by the Russians. Mrs. Peters, Katharina, Maria, Louise, and Henry's wife, Anna, went to Paraguay. There it was very difficult to settle. Anna, the wife of Henry Peters, along with her family, came to Winnipeg where I once visited them in 1954. Maria, the wife of Henry Braul, came to Vineland, Ontario, with her family. We visited them in 1974.

Henry died, as well as Jacob Funk and Henry Braul. And of the others I do not know. The old Mrs. Henry Peters died in Paraguay on February 24, 1967, at the age of 92.

Father's half brother, Johan Martens, was born in the village of Eliesabettal. He married ?? and moved then to the settlement of Stavropol. Father's half sister, Nella, was born in the village of Eliesabettal. Here she married David Koop and lived in that village. They were later deported.

Then Grandmother Martens had adopted a Russian girl. She grew up in the home of Grandmother Martens, went to school in the village of Eliesabettal, was baptized as a Mennonite and married ? Penner.

Appendix 5: Hoffnungsfeld Mennonite Church
(Grande Prairie, Alberta, Canada)
Source: Centre for MB Studies, Winnipeg, MB (NP052-02-052).

In the spring of 1926, a group of over a dozen families, including over 30 children and youth, settled in the Peace River area through the assistance of the Canadian Mennonite Board of Colonization, which helped the settlers purchase the Adair Ranch. The ranch consisted of 22 quarters of land, a large barn that could hold 100 horses, two houses, a blacksmith shop, and a pump house. The former owner, Henry Adair, assisted the newcomers for the first year in learning farming methods that were quite different than the methods they new. The group worked the land together for the first two years. In the early years there was much cooperation between the various Mennonite groups and joint services were often held at the Adair Ranch.

The church building in Wembley was constructed in the winter of 1928-29 and made of logs from the nearby bush. In Beaverlodge a similar church was constructed on the farmstead of Jakob Thiessen.

The Hoffnungsfeld Mennonite Church at Grande Prairie (*Hoffnungsfelder Mennoniten Gemeinde zu Grande Prairie*) was organized on July 30, 1927. The church was composed of local congregations that met in Wembley, Beaverlodge, and Lymburn. Elder Franz Enns of Whitewater, Manitoba, officiated at the organizational meeting. Jakob Thiessen from the Beaverlodge group was appointed to serve as leading minister, and Gerhard A. Neufeld from Wembley and Jacob D. Nickel from Lymburn also served as ministers. Neufeld and Nickel were ordained by Elder Cornelius D. Harder on June 30, 1929.

On June 27, 1931, J. D. Nickel became the elder of the church and was ordained on February 21, 1932. At this time the three congregations had a total membership of 115.[53]

The Hoffnungsfeld Mennonite Church in Beaverlodge
Source: Centre for MB Studies, Winnipeg, MB (NP052-02-052)

Appendix 6: Johann Neufeld, Obituary

Johan Neufeld, Obituary
Der Bote, Wednesday, November 24, 1993

Ältester Johan Neufeld   1905 – 1993
Calgary, Alberta (earlier Tofield)

The death of his saints is noteworthy before the Lord. I would like to set the words from Psalm 116 for the going home of brother Neufeld who entered eternity on October 14, 1993. During the years of his being here he often served with the Word until his health no longer permitted him to continue. The dear one who has gone home garnered great knowledge of the Bible through self study of the Holy Scriptures.

On October 18 the congregational leader, Herman Walde, greeted the mourners with word and prayer. A choir under the direction of Jacob Kroeger sang favourite songs of the family as well as of the congregation. Abe Bergen, leader of the Tofield congregation, remembered in a loving manner his esteemed work as Ältester (Elder) in service together with words from Psalm 40:1-10. All the words of recognition that followed showed how faithfully the deceased earned his daily bread with his own hands and did his church service without payment.

Brother Walde lifted words of comfort on the mourning widow, the children, and the grandchildren with the first verse from the 27th Psalm, "The Lord is my light." It was emphasised again and again, whether during happy or in sad times, that the Lord was his light on his life's journey. In God's hand brother Neufeld knew he was always safe and secure. His mortal shell was buried at the Queenspark cemetery. The funeral luncheon took place in the basement of our church. Preacher Rudy Janssen spoke words with reminiscences of the past 20 years after words from the Gospel of John 5:24. The get-together came to an end with a song and a prayer by Associate Pastor David Bergen.

Written for the family by Charlotte Wiehler

Biography

Johan Neufeld was born on June 6, 1905, in the village of Marienthal. His parents were Johan and Anna (Nachtigal) Neufeld. When he was seven, his mother died and Barbara Funk became his stepmother. He attended the village school in Marienthal and a school for advanced training in Alexandertal but, because of the Revolution and famine, he had to end his education. In 1924 his father died. Because he was the eldest sibling, much responsibility was laid on him. Upon his confession of faith in Jesus as his saviour he was baptized on June 2, 1925, in the Pordenau Church by Elder Aaron Regehr and became a member of the Pordenauer Mennonitengemeinde (Pordenau Mennonite Church).

In 1926 he emigrated to Canada with his stepmother and seven siblings. There they received a friendly reception from relatives in Colonsay, Saskatchewan. In 1927 they moved to Beaverlodge in the Grande Prairie district. During the following year (1928) they moved to a farm southwest of Beaverlodge near Rio Grande.

On June 27, 1931, he was called to be a minister in the Hoffnungsfelder Mennonite Church and on August 6, 1933, he was ordained as a minister by Elder Harder. In 1936, when Rev. Thiessen moved to British Columbia, he went to Beaverlodge and served the group there with the Word of God. Here he also found a wife in Liese (Louise) Enns and on August 6, 1939, they were married. For three more years, from 1939 to 1942, he served the congregation in Wembly with the Word of God. In addition, he was employed in his trade.

In 1942 he and his wife and their little daughter moved to Tofield, Alberta. Here he was immediately drawn into the congregation first as a Sunday school teacher and then as Sunday School Superintendent for eight years. He also assisted with preaching during this time. In 1955 he was called to be the leading minister in the Tofield Mennonite Church. For six years he had this duty and on May 7, 1961, he was chosen to be Ältester (Elder) of the Tofield Mennonite Church and was ordained on August 6. In 1973 he retired and moved with his wife to Calgary where most of his children lived.

Translation by Gerald Neufeld from the original German obituary

Appendix 7: John Neufeld's Original Handwritten Memoir, Pages 1 – 10

Was Ich Gesehen, Gehört
und Erlebt Habe

von

John Neufeld

1977

Grossvater Johan Gerhard Neufeld war geboren am 31 August 1833 in Preussen (Deutschland) Als er 6 Jahre alt war im Jahre 1839 wanderte seine Eltern mit ihm und seinem Bruder, der etwas jünger war als er aus nach Russland. In seinen alten Tagen hat er mir erzählt das er konnte sich erinnern von das Haus in welchen Sie gewohnt hatten auch etwas von der Reise wie sie mit Pferden und Wagen waren die lange Strecke gefahren.

In Russland kamen sie bis zur Molotschnaer Mennoniten Ansiedlung. Im Dorfe Elisabetthal blieben sie die erste Zeit vielleicht hatten seine Eltern da in dem Dorfe Verwanten Die Dörfer Mariental, Pordenau, Schardau, und Alexandertal waren schon Angesiedelt im Jahre 1820. Das Dorf Elisabettag erst im Jahr 1824.

Bald kaufte Grossvater sein Vater im Dorfe Mariental die Wirtschaft ~~Nummer~~ 10 welches zu meiner Zeit die Johan Martens Wirtschaft war. Im nächsten Dorfe Pordenau hate man eine Kirche gebaut so wurde auch die Gemeinde die Pordenauer Mennoniten Gemeinde genannt. Hier wird Grossvater und sein Bruder auch getauft und Glieder dieser Gemeinde

Als Grossvater 25 Jahre alt war trat er in dem Ehestand mit Katariena Wiens warscheinlich aus dem Dorfe Pordenau Katariena Wiens unsere Grossmutter war geboren am 24 Januar 1839. Bald darauf kauft Grossvater die Wirtschaft #5 an der nordseite der Strasse im Dorfe Mariental. Sein Bruder Gerhard kaufte, oder übernahm, die Wirtschaft welche sein Vater hatte. Ich kann mir erinnern das ich ihm in diesem Hause noch gesehen habe als ein alter Man schon über 75 Jahre alte

Weil Grossvater gut singen konnte und auch singen liebte wurde er bald in der Pordenauer Kirche zum Vorsanger gewählt das ist er muste die Lieder ansagen zum singen

Als er 41 Jahre alt war, im Jahr 1874 wurde er in der Pordenau Gemeinde zum Prediger berufen. Über 35 Jahre hat er in dieser Gemeinde als Prediger gearbeitet. Er war kein Gelehrter aber wie andere mir erzählt haben ein sehr Angesehener und ein beliebter Prediger. Zu meiner Zeit oder von die Zeit wo ich mir kan sinnen habe ich ihm schon nicht predigen gehört er war schon zu alt aber ich habe ihm gesehen jeden Sonntag sitzen in der Kirche wo die Prediger sasen

Der Herr schenkte Grossvater und Grossmutter 6 Kinder. Ich will sie hier aufschreiben so viel als ich gehört und gesehen habe von ihnen.

Katarina war die älteste Tochter (Vater seine Schwester sie war 6 Jahre älter als Vater) sie war geboren am 24 Januar 1862. Als sie 22 Jahre alt war im Jahre 1884 den 27 May verheiratete sie sich mit Peter Gorz. Er war des Nachbars Sohn. Er war Lehrer mehrere Jahre in einem Mennonitischen Dorf auf der Halbinsel Krim. Als im Jahre 1890 die Molotschna Kolonie in der Provinz Samara Land kaufte für ihre Landlose und da 12 Dörfer gründeten gingen Peter Gorzens dorthin! Für eine kurze Zeit war er auch da Lehrer. Dann gab er den Lehrerberuf auf. Kaufte eine Wirtschaft, ich denke im Dorfe Podolsk und wurde Bauer. Die Ansiedlung wählte ihm da aber zum Waisenmann das heist er sollte die Waisenkinder wo Vater und Mutter gestorb waren ihr Geld verwalten bis sie 21 Jahre alt waren, dann konnten sie selbiges erhalten. Hier in Podolk war auch die Mennoniten Brudergemeinde ihre Kirche. Peter Gorzen schlossen sich hier die Brudergemeinde an

Der Herr schenkte ihnen 7 Kinder von welche ich den ältesten Sohn Peter und die jüngste Tochter Sara gesehen habe. Sara arbeitete als Krankenschwester (Nurse) in der Anstalt Betania in der Alten Kolonie. Im Jahre 1921 war sie bei uns zu besuch

Dan Peter der älteste Sohn sah ich zum ersten Mal im Jahr 1938 in Linbrok wo er mit seiner Familie damals wohnte. Als junger Man wolte er Missionar werden er ging nach Deutschland studierte da Teologie in Berlin. Ehe der 1 Weltkrieg ausbracht kam er zurück und konnte nicht mehr zurück nach Deutschland um weiter zu lernen. Er verheiratete sich mit Maria Foot. Sie wanderten im Jahre 1924 oder 25 aus nach Canada. Bei Crowfoot farmte er mehrere Jahre. Als es in den drüsiger Jahre da sehr troken war zogen sie nach Linbrook wo er auch eine Farm hatte. Schon in Russland war er in der Mennoniten Brudergemeinde zum Prediger berufen worden und hier hat er dann auch viel für den Herrn gearbeitet. Er hatte eine grosse Familie, hatte auch manches Schwere in der Familie mit etliche von seinen Söhnen. Im Jahre 1956 starb ihm seine Frau. Seine zweite Frau war Anna Dick von Pinchu Creek Seine Farm verkaufte er an seinen Sohn Ab und zog nach Edmonton wo er im Ruhestand lebte. Im Jahr 1972 starb auch diese Frau. Bald darauf ging er nach St. Catarins Oht im Manor Altenheim wo im Feb. 1974 ich ihn noch besuchte er war dann schon 88 Jahre alt. Er starb am 14 May 1976 in St. Katarinas und wurde am 18 May bei Tofield (Linbrook) begraben

Dan der zweite Sohn Herrman er war etwas älter als Vater. Von dem hat man wenig gesprochen. Als ich Vater mal fragte wie es kam das seine Schwester Katarina 6 Jahre älter war als er sagte er da war ein Bruder zwischen Katarina und ihm gewesen der aber ertrunken war als kleiner Junge

Dann war Vater geboren im Jahr 1868 am 16 September von ihm werde ich später seh
Vater seine andere Schwester Maria war geboren am 3 July 1870.
1895 den 6 June hatte sie Hochzeit gehabt mit Abram Heidebrecht von Hamberg. Er
war Witwer, hatte mehrere Kinder 6 oder 7 etliche waren schon erwachsen. Wie
ich gehört habe war er auch 20 Jahre älter als sie. Sie hatten dann noch 3 Kinder
zusammen Neta Gerhard und Dietrich. Ich kann mich erinnern das zu
Weihnachten und Ostern sie nach Hause zu uns kamen, Abram Heidebrecht tat
sehr an Asthma leiden. Ich weiß nicht in welchem Jahre 1916 oder 1917 eines Sonntag als Va
und Grossvater aus der Kirche nach Hause kamen waren bei uns 2 Man von dem Dorfe Ha
bach, es war Winter sie waren auf dem Schlitten gekommen, sie sagten das Abram Heideb
und seine Frau beide gestorben waren. Er war über Mittag an Asthma gestorben sie he
die Flu gehabt, aber hatte noch alles geregelt wie es sollte auf dem Begräbnis se
und des Nacht war auch sie gestorben. Vater und Grossvater fuhren zum
Begräbnis und ich konnte auch mitfahren. Das Begräbnis war im Hause, da
standen zwei Sarge und auf dem Kirchhof wurden sie auch beidzusamen in
ein Grab gelassen. Wo sollten die drei Kinder jetzt bleiben? die andern von seiner
ersten Frau waren schon alle verheiratet. Dann nahm Gerhard Neufeld Vater sein
jüngerer Bruder der im Dorfe Paulsheim wohnte und eine grosse Familie hatte
die drei auch noch hin. Neta heiratete bald einen Jacob Fransen aus dem selben
Dorfe und Gerhard heiratet eine ? Ediger auch aus dem Dorfe. Dietrich
lernte wurde Lehrer im Dorfe Herzenberg. Während des zweiten Weltkrieges kam
er mit seine Familie ausein ander. Seine Frau wurde zurück nach Russland
geschickt. Er und ein Sohn kamen nach Paraguay dann später auch nach
Canada, Ont. wo ich ihm im Jahre 1962 noch besuchte. Seine Frau durfte auch
noch von Russland herauskommen. Doch, wie ich gehört habe, sie hatten sich aus
ein ander gelebt. Er starb bald darauf.

Weiter war Vater seine jüngst Schwester Aganetha sie war geboren im Jahr 1874
den 14 Mai. Diese verheiratete sich mit Peter Voth auch aus dem Dorf Hamberg
das war im Jahr 1898 den 15 Januar hatten sie Hochzeit und am 8 Oktober
bekamen sie einen Sohn Hans sie war dann aber krank und am 5 Dezember
starb sie des Begräbnis war am 9 December 1898. Peter Voth heiratete wieder
wohnte später im Dorf Alexandertal, sie hatten noch 5 andere Kinder. Weil Peter
Voth kein Land eignete, er tat meistens ausschafen, so tat er Hans in Alexander
krone in der hohen Schule gehen, lernen welche er auch beendigte. Während die
Revolutionszeit ging er mit die weise Arme mit. Für eine längere Zeit wussten
seine Eltern nichts von ihm. Als ich im Jahr 1920 in Alexantertal zur Schule
ging kam er mit einmal nach Hause. Er war bei die rote Arme in Gefangen-
schaft gekommen. Als er nach Hause kam war er oder seine Kleider sehr zerrissen

und er war sehr verlaust. Er wurde sehr bereinigt aber er bekam bald Zyfos. Er bekehrte sich dann und er wurde auch wieder gesund. Seine Bekehrung war aber nicht gründlich gewesen. Bald wurde er im Dorfe Alexandertal in der Sowjetoffice als Sekretär angestellt wurde dann aber getransfert nach dem Russenulbofe Jakmati wo er auch Sekretär war. Hier wurde er mit ein jüdisches Mädchen bekannt welches er dann auch heiratete. Ich habe gehört das er sich der Sowjet communistische Idea zuneigte.

Vater sein junger Bruder Gerhard war geboren am 4 März, 1872. Er war einer der auch den Forstdienst dienen musste. In Maria Friessen Pauliheim fand er seine Ehegattin am 11 Januar 1901 hatten sie Hochzeit. Da Friessens nur die Maria als einziges Kind hatte so tat Gerhard nach die Hochzeit auch die Wirtschaft über nehmen. Er war auch sehr erfolgreich in der Wirtschaft und als Bauer. Der Herr schenkte ihme 8 Kinder, 5 Söhne und 3 Tochter. Er hielt auch sehr darauf das seine Jungens sollten weiter lernen. Im Jahre 1926 als wir auswanderten, wollte er mit seine Familie auch auswandern. Er hatte auch alles fertig, die Pässe, die Medikal vom Dr. auch seine Wirtschaft hatte er schon verkauft. An einen bestimmten Tage war auch der Ausruf mit das andere was sie hatte. Beim Ausruf hatten sie auch ganz schön eingenommen da kamen des Nachts als sie sich zur Ruhe gelegt hatten etliche Mann Räuber, Es war im August und weil es im Hause etwas warm war schlief Willy einer von den Jungens draussen vor der Tür auf eine Bank. Diesem taten die Räuber da zu erst schlagen, der schrie, sein Vater, Onkel Gerhard Neufeld horte das, er öffnete das Fenster sprang heraus um seinen Sohn zu helfen. Einer von der Räuber schoss und die Kugel ging ihm durch die Brust. Die Räuber, die verschwanden dann ohne das sie etwas Geld bekommen hatten. Die Jungens fuhren mit ihrem Vater noch nach Muntau zum Hospital aber er war schon tot als sie hin kamen.
Das Bigrabniss war ein paar Tage dann wanderten die Jungens mit ihre Mutter und alle Geschwister auch der Alte Grossvater Friessen aus nach Canada. Gerhard einer von den Jungens war schon paar Monate früher ausgewandert. Zuerst kamen sie nach Kitchener Ont dann zogen sie nach Vineland Ont. Gerhard hatt sich schon in Russland verheiratet, Cornelius, Willy, Peter, und Susie verheirateten sich in Ont. Johan Mary und Kathy aber sind allein geblieben. Bald nachdem sie hier nach Canada kamen in Vineland starb der alte Grossvater Friessen dann auch noch etliche Jahre die Mutter. Johan Mary und Kathy haben immer zusammen gewohnt erst auf einer Farm dann als sie die Farm verkauften, taten sie retiren und wohnen in Vineland. Cornelius und Gerhard die auch jeder eine grosse Farm hatten sind auch schon retiert. Willy bearbeitet noch seine Farm so auch Peter. Susie die einen Peter Dyck geheiratet hatty wohnte bei Dunville Ont auf eine Farm. Im Jahre 1974 im Februar war

Jetzt von meinem Vater. Er war geboren im Dorfe Marietal im Jahre 1868 am 16 Sep
hier ging er auch zur Schule, die Schule war damals noch sehr einfach so auch der
Unterricht so das Vater nicht viel Bildung hatte. In der Fordenauer Kirche wo Gross
vater Prediger war wurde er auch getauft. Als er 23 Jahre alt war wurde er bekannt
mit Helena Bekker aus dem Dorfe Schardau. Wie es damals Sitte und Gebrauch war
so hatte er seinen Vater gefragt ob er würde mal nach Bekker fahren und fragen
ob die würden ihm die Helena zur Frau geben. Grossvater war dan hin gefahren
nach Bekkers und die hatten das gerne getan. Sie hatten sich dan geeinigt das
die Verlobung (engagement) am 30 Okt 1899 sein solte und die Hochzeit war dan am
12 Nov. 1899. Helena Bekker war geboren am 7 April 1872
Vater nahm seine junge Frau und wohnte dan bei Grossvater in der Sommerstube. Unser Haus will ich hier etwas beschreiben. Wen wir von der Vordertür herein kamen
war zu erst das Vorderhaus dan zur linken Hand war die Sommerstube und zur rechten
Hand war die grosse Stube (oder Zimmer) Mitten im Haus war eine Wand. Aus der grossen
Stube ging man dan in die Ekstube diese wurde meistens gebraucht als Schlafzimmer
während die grosse Stube das Gestzimmer war. Aus der Ekstube ging man in die
kleine Stube welche auch als Schlafzimmer und auch als Familienzimmer
gebracht wurde. Dan ging man aus der kleine Stube im Hinterhaus. Diese lag
dem dem Vorderhaus und die Sommerstube gegenüber. Dazwischen war die kleine
Küche wo gekocht und gebraten wurde. Aus dem Hinterhaus war eine Tür zum hin
aus gehen. Dan waren bei dem Hinterhaus noch zwei kleine Kamern, die eine war
die Pantry aus welche man auch im Keller gehen konnte, die andere war eine
Kamer wo man oft Schinkel und anderes Fleisch aufbewahrte. Aus dem Hinterhaus war auch eine Tür die zum Stall führte. Der Stall war am Haus an
gebaut
Vater wohnte dan wie ich schon geschrieben habe mit seine junge Frau Helena in
der Sommerstube. Er bearbeite dan Grossvater seine Wirterhaft
Ich will jetzt nieder schreiben was Vater selber in em Buch geschrieben hat das ich
heute noch lesen kan. Am Morgen den 13 November 1900 ist meine liebe
Helena krank geworden und erst am 16 Nov. ist sie mit unsagbaren grossen
Schmerzen von einem toten Söhnchen entbunden worden. Sie war hiernach
aber so schwach das wir glaubten sie würde den Abend schon nicht erleben
Sie wurde aber noch etwas starker. Wir haben uns dan noch viel besprochen
und viel gebetet und so ist sie nach 4 wöchentliche Krankheit ruhig im
Glauben an ihrem Heiland gestorben. So weit was Vater geschrieben hatte
Vater hat mir einmal erzählt als sie schon in den letzten Stunde gelegen
hatte und sie um ihr Sterbebett gestanden hatte und wo sie geglaubt
hatten jetzt war sie schon tot dan hatte sie noch einmal die Augen aufge-
tan ihm gewinkt er sollte näher kommen und dan hatte sie noch gesagt

sie hatte schon etwas sehr schönes sehr herrliches gesehen, sie konnte aber nicht mit Worten sagen was es war viel zu schön, sie wolte nur dahin gehen was sie gesehen und gehört hatte. Vater sagte sie hatte die himmlische Herrlichkeit gesehen. Als sie das gesagt hatte war sie gestorben. Am 10 Dezember 1900 war das Begräbnis

4 Jahre war Vater Witwer (widower) dan trat er mit Anna Nachtigal in dem Ehestande Vater hat mir einmal erzählt wie der liebe Gott ihm unsere Mama zu geführt hatte Als einmal sein gewesener Schwiegervater Peter Bekker (Schardau) bei seinem Bruder Heinrich Bekker im Dorfe Rudnerweide spazieren war dan hatte Heirich Bekker gefragt Nun und die Helena ihr Man Johan Neufeld ist der schon verheiratt? Nein hatte Peter Bekker gesagt. Na der solte doch kommen die Anna Nachtigal heiraten hatte Heinrich Bekker gesagt. Nur war Anna Nachtigal? Heinrich Bekker seine Frau ihr Bruder Peter Nachtigal dem war die Frau gestorben. Er hatte drei Kinder Peter, Heinrich und Anna. Er verheiratete sich wieder aber nach eine kurze Zeit starb er. Seine Frau die sich dan wieder verheiraten wolte, wolte aber nicht diese drei Kinder haben. Wo sollten die jetzt bleiben. Ein Weisenhaus so wie später eins war im Dorfe Grossweide war damals noch nicht. Jemand nahm die zwei Jungens mit nach der Provinz Ufa. Anna aber kam zu ihrem Onkel Heinrich Nachtigal der im Dorfe Franstal wohnte. Nur aber fand Anna unsere Mama aber nicht Elteren liebe. Diese hatten eine Tochter die immer vorgezogen wurde. Anna Nachtigal die mehr klein von Gewächs war muste aber immer mehr die schwere Arbeit tun Als bei Gelegenheit Heinrich Bekker mit Anna Nachtigal gesprochen hatte ob sie würde wollen mit einen Johan Neufeld in den Ehestand treten dan hatte sie sich sehr gefreut Johan Bekker hatte bei Gelegenheit mit unsern Vater davon gesprochen. Als Vater dan mal hin fuhr nach Anna Nachtigal dan hatte er gleich gewust das ist die die der Herr für ihn hatte. Am 12 Juni 1904 hatten sie Verlobung und am 23 Juni Hochzeit. So war Vater und unsere Mama zusammen gekommen.

Mama war geboren am 5 Feb 1881 im Dorfe Rudnerweide Sie war 23 Jahre alt als sie sich verheiratete, Vater war 36 Jahre alt. Vater und Mama wohnten wieder bei Grossvater in der Sommerstube. Mama war im ganz armes Mädchen gewesen aber sie hatte bei Vater ein Heim gefunden und Vater und Mama waren sehr glücklich. Grossvater und Grossmutter waren auch sehr gut zu ihr

Ich wurde geboren am 6 Juni 1905 und meine Schwester Maria ist geboren am 28 Oktober 1906. Im Jahre 1908 den 19 August ist mein Bruder Peter geboren Dan am 26 Feb. 1909 starb Grossmutter nachdem sie etwas über 70 Jahre alt war Ich kan mir wenig von Grossmutter erinnern. Nur von dem Begräbnis. Das Begräbnis war im Hause ich war aber krank muste in der Sommerstube im Bett bleiben   Vater hat in ein Buch geschrieben folgendes

Im Jahre 1907 im Oktober fuhr einmal nach der Ansiedlung Samara seine Schwester

Katharina Frau Peter George besuchen. Der Grund aber war nicht nur der Besuch sondern er wolte da wen möglich eine Wirtschaft kaufen. Bis jetzt hatte Vater nur immer für Grossvater gearbeitet. Er hatte schon eine Familie er wolte auch etwas eigenes haben. Von Grossvater wolte er die halbe Wirtschaft kaufen aber das wolte der nicht. Als Vater von Samara zurück kam dem müste Grossvater jetzt war es Zeit wen er ihm jetzt nicht die halbe Wirtschaft verkaufte dan wurde Vater weg ziehen. So kaufte Vater dan die halbe Wirtschaft und bearbeitete die ganze Wirtschaft das hatt auch Grossvater sein Teil. Von dieser Reise nach Samara hat Vater uns erzählt. Er und noch 3 oder 4 andere Männer aus unserm Dorfe waren dahin gefahren. Sie fuhren mit dem Zuge bis zur Station Sorotchinski. Da nahmen sie einen Russischen Fuhrman an der ihnen bis zur Ansiedlung bringen solte. Es war wohl noch 4 oder 5 Stunden zu fahren mit Pferde. Es wurde Abend es schneite der Wind wurde immer stärker. Mit einmal war ein starker Blissart. Die Pferde gingen immer langsamer. Mit einmal hatte der Fuhrman gesagt. Jetzt sind wir verirrt. Das meinte das sie dan auch konnten da auf der Steppe tot frieren. Dan hatten sie sich alle da beim Schlitten im Schnee nieder gekniet und hatte ernstlich Gebett auch der russische Fuhrman. Und als sie auf gestanden waren hatten sie ein kleines Licht gesehen sie waren dan dahin gefahren und bald waren sie im warmen Haus Vater glaubte an Gebetserhörungen.

1910 den 23 Oktober ist meine Schwester Anna geboren.   Im Jahre 1912 Dan im Januar oder Februar wurde unsere Mama krank. Der Doktor sagte sie solte eine innerliche Operation haben. Vater brachte ihr nach Muntau zum Hospital. Vater der fuhr dan jeden andern Tag hin. Einmal wohl noch vor der Operation hatte Mama zu Vater gesagt, ob er nicht könnte mich mitbringen, sie wolte mir noch einmal sehen. Den nächsten Tag fuhr Vater wieder hin und ich fuhr auch mit. Es war sehr kalt. Wir fuhren mit dem Verdeck feederwagen. Kamen da gegen Abend hin. Mama lag ganz weis angezogen im Bett. Ich sas bei ihr am Bett und sie hielt meine Hand. Ich weis noch das die Nursen auch für mich Abendbrot brachten und ich ass da bei Mama ihr Bett. Auch brachten die Nursen mir noch ein Bilderbuch. Vater hatte da auf eine andere Stelle Nacht quartier, die Nursen aber wolten haben ich solte da im Hospietal, im Hallway in ein schönes Bett schlafen, was ich dan auch tat. Den andern Tag fuhren wir wieder nach Hause. Vater holte auch unse Mama nach etliche Wochen nach Hause. Nicht das sie ganz gesund von der operation war aber sie wurde immer gesünder. Im Sommer war sie wieder ganz gesund. Dan kam der 21 August. Vater tat mit russische Arbeiter in der Scheune Getreide rein machen Mama mit ein Dienstmädchen taten Wäsche waschen dan am Nachmittag wurde Mama krank (sie hatte eine Miscarige) Vater hatt in ein Buch geschrieben, ich holte auch gleich die Hebame (Mitwife) Mama war aber noch bis Abend auf dan wurde sie sehr krank. In Nacht musten wir kinder und Gross- vater schon in der Sommerstube schlafen. Nach Grossmutter ihren Tode waren

waren Vater und Mama mit uns Kinder in die kleine Stube gezogen. Diese Nacht sollten
wir aber wieder in der Sommerstube schlafen. Ich konnte nicht schlafen. Licht war
im ganzen Hause, auf und ab wurde gegangen, ich hörte das auf dem Hof gefahren
wurde. Vater hat des Nachts den Doktor geholt, dieser tat was er konnte, aber ihre
Stunde war gekommen. Gegen Morgen am 22 August war sie gestorben. Des Morgens
noch ehe die Sonne aufgegangen war kam Vater in die Sommerstube, ich und
meine Schwester Maria zogen uns an, er nahm uns bei der Hand ging mit uns
bis zur kleinen Stuben Tür. Da blieb er stehen, wir schauten herein. Da lag unsere
Mama auf dem Bett, die Augen zu, sie tat auch nicht mehr atmen. Sie war
gestorben. Ich kann mir denken wieviel sie noch in dieser letzten
Nacht für mich und meine andern Geschwister gebetet wird haben.
Jetzt muste Mama besorgt werden. Am 22 August war das Begräbniss bei
uns in der grossen Scheune. Ich weis noch, Mama lag im Sarg. Vater wir
Kinder und Grossvater sassen dicht beim Sarge. Es waren auch viele Menschen
zum Begräbniss gekommen. Von der Predigt weis ich nicht viel, ich weis aber das
man schöne Lieder sangen. Der Sarg wurde zum Kirchhof getragen, wir gingen
hinter dem Sarge. Dort wurde der Sarg in die Erde gelassen und dann zuge-
schaufelt. Wir hatten jetzt keine Mama mehr.
Tante Maria Frau Heidebrecht nahm meine Schwester Anna die nur etwas über anderthalb
Jahre alt mit zu ihr. Vater nahm eine altere Frau an als Hauskeeper. Die machte das Essen
hielt das Haus in Ordnung und besorgte uns 3 Kinder. Anna war ja bei ihre Tante Maria
Anfangs September fing ich an nach Schule zu gehen. Mein Lehrer war jetzt Co. Wiens
Einmal als der Lehrer mit uns alle Schüler singen tat, war es mir als wen ich die schöne
Lieder hörte die man bei Mama ihr Begräbnis gesungen hatte und es war als wen ich ihr sah
im Sarge noch liegen. Ich fing an zu weinen. Der Lehrer fragte was mir war. Ich sagte
aber nichts dann sagte der Lehrer ob ich wolte nach Hause gehen. Zu Hause fragte Vater mir
was mir war, ich sagte es ihm dann alles. Nach etliche Tage hatte der Lehrer Vater gefragt
und Vater hatte ihm dann alles gesagt. Ich merkte es das so was bei ihm konnte sein hatte
der Lehrer gesagt.
Es war im Januar 1913 eines Abends (es war bei uns Sitte damals das wir um 12 Uhr Mittag
essen dann um 4 Uhr Vesper und um 9 Uhr Abendbrot diese Sitte wurde später abgetan
oft waren wir Kinder dann schon zu schläfrig zum Abendbrot essen, wir essen dann
schon früher und gingen schlafen) an diesem Abend im Januar Monat hatte man
gebakte Kartoffeln, die schmeckten mir besonders gut. Ich blieb auf um mit Vater
Grossvater und die Andern Abendbrot zu essen. Vater und ich sassen beim Essen
da sagte Vater mit einmal "Hans was denkst du wen ich mir wieder eine
Mama suchte für euch." Ich weis nicht ob ich etwas sagte aber ich freute mir sehr
In Barbara Funk aus dem Dorfe Mariawohl fand Vater wieder eine Frau und Mutter
für uns Kinder. Doch ehe sie Vater das Jawort gab wolte sie doch die Kinder sehen die sie

sich übernehmen sollte. Vater brachte sie eines Tages zu uns. Ich weis noch wie sie sas auf
eine Stuhl und sagte, wir sollten mal zu ihr kommen – Sie nahm uns bei der Hand und
streichelte uns. Sie wurde unsere Mutter und sie ward eine gute Mutter für uns Kinder.
Ich werde ihr hier nennen Mutter zum Unterschiede von unsre Mama!
Am 24 Januar 1913 hatte Vater und Mutter Verlobung und den 9 Feb Hochzeit. Diese Hochzeit
war bei ihre Eltern im Hause. Am Abend vor der Hochzeit war, wie es Sitte damals
war, der Polterabend (ein Schauer) wo dem Brautpaar viele Geschenke gegeben wurde.
Die Jugend hatte auch viele Gedichte aufgesagt auch etliche Plays gebracht. Unter
dem Die sich besonders hervor getan hatte mit Gedichte aufsagen war der Lehrer Johan
Wichert. Der heute noch lebt, er ist schon über 88 Jahr alt, viele Jahre war er Ältester
der Tienlander Mennoniten Gemeinde. Heute ist er retiert. Wir Kinder waren nicht bei der Hochz.
Mutter kam mehr aus eine wohlhabende Familie während unsere Mama eine ganz arme
war. Sie bekam auch von ihre Eltern die volle Ausstattung, die verschiedenste Möbeln so
auch ein Pferd und anderes mehr. Mutter war geboren am 16 Dezember 1882.
Vater war ein ganzer Bauer. Er sagte Mal wen der Pflug die Erde umdrehte der Geruch
von der Erde liebte er. Jetzt wurden im Hause verschiedene Änderungen gemacht.
In der grossen Stube wurde Lenoleum gelegt und anderes mehr. Der Stall
und die grosse Scheune wurden mit Schindeln gedeckt. Die Maschine mit welche
Getreide geschnitten wurde (Lobogreyka) wurde bei Seite gestellt. Vater kaufte eine andere
die Harkmaschine zum Getreide schneiden. Anstatt im Frühling dem Sommer –
weizen zu säken, der nicht viel vom Acker einbrachte. Kaufte Vater sich eine
neue Art Winterweizen (Bernothy) der sehr viel mehr vom Acker einbrachte als der
Sommerweizen. Vater war auch im Begriff einen Selbstbinder zu kaufen
wo das Getreide in Garben gebunden wurde. Auch dachte Vater schon an einen
Motor zu kaufen zum Getreide dreschen. Er tat auch nicht mehr Sonnenblume
oder Korn pflanzen, das sagte er war zu hart für das Land. Er machte aber
mehr Schwarzbrache (Sommerfolow) und tat diese gut und mehremal pflügen, er
wollte damit die Feuchtigkeit in die Erde halten. So war Vater in allem fort-
schrittlich gesinnen. Auch in unserm Dorfe war Vater einer von den fortschritt-
lichsten Bauer.
Da kam der Augustmonat 1914 wo der erste Weltkrieg ausbrach. Mit diesem
kam manches zu Ende. Ich erinnere mich noch wie wir anfangs August mit
die letzte Getreide fuhren vom Felde kamen wie ich hörte des Nachbars russischer
Arbeiter zu unserm Arbeiter rief: Morgen fahren wir zum Krieg.
Anfänglich merkten wir wenig davon. Die junge Manns aus unserm
Dorfe wurden einer nach dem andern eingezogen. Als Mennoniten durften
sie nicht mit Gewehren auf die Front sein aber sie musten dienen
als Sanitäter (Krankenpfleger) in Hospitäler wo die verwundete Soldaten geheilt
wurden dan auch auf den Zügen die die verwundete Soldaten von der Front

nach Moskau und ander Städten brachten. Auch etliche von den besten Pferden aus unsere Dorfe, so auch aus jedem andern Dorfe, nahm die Regirung tat aber gut dafür bezah. Ihmer mehr von den jungen Manner wurden zum Kriege im berufen auch unser Lehrer Cor. Wiens wurde eingezogen. Die junge Lehrer mit Bildung waren jetzt knapp. Man nahm schliesslich einen alten Lehrer Friessen als Lehrer an. Er war schon über 60 Jahre alt, hatte auch nicht die Bildung konnte auch nicht mehr Deceplin in der Schule halten. Wir lernten auch nicht viel von ihm. Dan im Herbst 1915 horte man mit einmal das der Kaiser im Begriff vor alle Deutschsprachige und alle Deutsche nach Sibirien zu evakuiren. Das gab dan viel Gedanken bei unsre Eltern. Auch wurde in dieser Zeit verboten öffentliche Versamlungen abzuhalten in der deutschen Sprache. Sogar in der Kirche kan ich mir erinnern wurde für kurze Zeit keine deutsche Predigt gebracht. Die Diakonen taten dan eine deutsche Predigt vorlesen. In der Schule hatte der Lehrer auch kein Weihnachts abend mit die Kinder.
Diese Furcht verschickt zu werden kam zum Abschluss im Jahre 1917 als in Moscow eine andere Regirung entstand. Der Kaiser muste zuruck tretten. Anfänglich war eine provisorische Regirung mit Kerensky an der Spitze. Aber diese konnte sich auch nicht lange halten, dan kam Lenin an die Regirung.
1913 den 23 Nov. ist meine Schwester Agnes geboren
1915 den 23 Nov ist mein Bruder Gerhard (Georgi) geboren
1917 den 21 Nov. ist mein Bruder Heinrich (Henry) geboren
Bald nachdem der Kaiser zuruck getretten war horte auch der Krieg mit Deutschland auf. Jetzt kamen auch die Manner aus unserm Dorfe die als Sanitäter und die die auf andern Stellen eingezogen waren und dienen musten einer nach dem andern nach hause. Durch in Abkommen mit die Regirung in Moscow tat das deutsche Militär die Ukraina besetzen. Das war wohl im Feb Monat 1917 jedoch die blieben nicht lange. Weil in Deutschland auch eine Revolution anfing, wo die Kaiser Regirung in Deutschland auch zuruck trat, zog das Deutsche Militär zuruck wohl im Oktober oder November Monat. Weil in der Ukraena keine Regirung war, entstanden bald viele Banden. Einer von den hervorragensten Führer dieser Banden war Nestor Machno. Diese raubten, plünderten, brannten und erschossen viele von den Grossfarmern. Auch viele von unsern Mennoniten die auf Farmen wohnten, ausserhalb unsern mennonitischen Ausiedlingen (Dorfer) wurden erschossen andere flüchteten und kamen bis unsre Dorfer.
Als das deutsche Militär im Oktober zuruck zog blieben etliche von diesen Soldaten zuruck, diese fingen auch gleich an in unsre Dorfer den Selbschutz zu organisiren. So sehr als auch unsere Mennonitische Prediger dagegen arbeiteten bald ging jeder junge Man mit ein Gewehr herum um unsre Dorfer zu schützen vor den Banden

[1] Alistair MacLeod, *No Great Mischief* (Toronto: McClelland & Stewart, Ltd.,1999), 97.

[2] As stated in the *Constitutional Act of 1867* between Britain and Canada.

[3] Cornelius J. Dyck, *An Introduction to Mennonite History, 3rd ed.* (Waterloo, Ontario: Herald Press, 1993), 31.

[4] New International Version Study Bible

[5] Dyck, *Mennonite History*, 45.

[6] Hugo Peters, *History and Hindsight, II. "Roots"* (Winnipeg, 2009-2016), 2

[7] Frank H. Epp, *Mennonite Exodus: the Rescue and Resettlement of the Russian Mennonites Since the Communist Revolution* (Altona, Manitoba: D. W Friesen & Sons Ltd., 1962), 13, 14.

[8] Peters, *"Roots,"* 2.

[9] Ibid, 2.

[10] "Russian Mennonite," Wikipedia, https://en.wikipedia.org/wiki/Russian_Mennonite#Migration_to_Russia.

[11] David G Rempel, *A Mennonite Family in Tsarist Russia and the Soviet Union, 1789 – 1923* (Toronto: University of Toronto Press, 2002), 5.

[12] Rempel, *A Mennonite Family*, 263.

[13] Harry Loewen, *No Permanent City: Stories from Mennonite History and Life* (Waterloo, Ontario: Herald Press, 1993), 116.

[14] Ibid, 123.

[15] Frank H. Epp, *Mennonite Exodus*, 27.

[16] Arthur Kroeger, *Hard Passage: A Mennonite Family's Long Journey from Russia to Canada* (Edmonton, The University of Alberta Press), 13.

[17] Statistics are cited by Cornelius J. Dyck, *An Introduction to Mennonite History, 3rd ed.* (Waterloo, Ontario, Herald Press, 1993), 182. Statistics cited are attributed to Al Reimer, "Peasant Aristocracy: The Mennonite *Gutsbesitzertum* in Russia," *Journal of Mennonite Studies*, vol. 8, 1990.

[18] Dyck, *Mennonite History*, 182, 183.

[19] Ibid, 14.

[20] Ibid, 212.

[21] Edgar Rogalski, translator and editor, *Diary of Johann Neufeld and Barbara Funk Neufeld: From Russian Revolution to Pioneer Life in Peace River, Alberta* (2009), 1,2.

[22] Kroeger, *Hard Passage*, 76,77.

[23] Ibid, 78.

[24] Victor Peters & Jack Thiessen, *Mennonite Names* (Marburg: N. G. Elwert Verlag, 1987), 94.

[25] Thiessen, Richard D. "Klein Lichtenau (Pomeranian Voivodeship, Poland)." *Global Anabaptist Mennonite Encyclopedia Online*. December 2012.

[26] Helmut T. Huebert, *Molotschna Historical Atlas* (Winnipeg, Springfield Publishers, 2003), 159.

[27] Ibid, 173.

[28] Encyclopedia Brittanica, https://www.britannica.com/topic/kulak

[29] Ibid, 161.

[30] Ibid, 161.

[31] Rogalski, *Diary of Johann Neufeld and Barbara Funk Neufeld, 10.*

[32] Rudy P. Friesen and Sergey Shmakin, *Into the Past: Buildings of the Mennonite Commonwealth* (Winnipeg: Raduga Publications, 1996), 252-253.

[33] Horst Gerlach, *Bildband zur Geschichte der Mennoniten* (Druck und verlag Günther Preuschoff, Oldenstadt, 1980), 84.

[34] https://en.wikipedia.org/wiki/Nestor_Makhno

[35] Rempel, *A Mennonite Family in Tsarist Russia*, 186.

[36] Ibid, 252, 253.

37 "A hundred years of immigration to Canada 1900 – 1999," Canadian Council for Refugees, https://ccrweb.ca/en/hundred-years-immigration-canada-1900-1999, May 2000.

38 Kroeger, *Hard Passage*, 96.

39 Epp, *Mennonite Exodus*, 344, 347.

40 Kroeger, *Hard Passage*, 169.

41 Ibid, 166-170.

42 Rogalski, *Diary*, 4.

43 Peter New, "Atlantic Park" *Eastleigh and District Historical Society, Occasional Paper No. 49.*

44 Epp, *Mennonite Exodus,* 171.

45 Ibid, 172.

46 Becky Taylor, "Immigration, Statecraft and Public Health: The 1920 Aliens Order, Medical Examinations and the Limitations of the State in England," *Social History of Medicine* (August 2016): Vol.29/3.

47 Epp, *Mennonite Exodus*, 173.

48 Centre for Mennonite Brethren Studies, Winnipeg, MB (NP052-02-052).

49 Global Anabaptist Mennonite Encyclopedia Online, https://gameo.org/index.php?title=Hoffnungsfeld_Mennonite_Church_(Grande_Prairie,_Alberta,_Canada).

50 New International Version

51 Anne Applebaum, "Ukraine and the Words that Lead to Mass Murder," *Atlantic*, April 15, 2022. (https://www.anneapplebaum.com/2022/04/25/ukraine-and-the-words-that-lead-to-mass-murder/)

52 "A hundred years of immigration to Canada 1900 – 1999" *Canadian Council for Refugees*, (https://ccrweb.ca/en/hundred-years-immigration-canada-1900-1999, May 2000).

53 Richard D. Thieseen, "Hoffnungsfeld Mennonite Church (Grande Prairie, Alberta, Canada)." *Global Anabaptist Mennonite Encyclopedia Online*. June 2013. Retrieved 2 Apr 2021. https://gameo.org/index.php?title=Hoffnungsfeld_Mennonite_Church_(Grande_Prairie,_Alberta,_Canada)&oldid=168356.

Endnotes

[1] Alistair MacLeod, *No Great Mischief* (Toronto: McClelland & Stewart, Ltd.,1999), 97.

[2] As stated in the *Constitutional Act of 1867* between Britain and Canada.

[3] Cornelius J. Dyck, *An Introduction to Mennonite History, 3rd ed.* (Waterloo, Ontario: Herald Press, 1993), 31.

[4] New International Version Study Bible

[5] Dyck, *Mennonite History*, 45.

[6] Hugo Peters, *History and Hindsight, II. "Roots"* (Winnipeg, 2009-2016), 2

[7] Frank H. Epp, *Mennonite Exodus: the Rescue and Resettlement of the Russian Mennonites Since the Communist Revolution* (Altona, Manitoba: D. W Friesen & Sons Ltd., 1962), 13, 14.

[8] Peters, *"Roots,"* 2.

[9] Ibid, 2.

[10] "Russian Mennonite," Wikipedia, https://en.wikipedia.org/wiki/Russian_Mennonite#Migration_to_Russia.

[11] David G Rempel, *A Mennonite Family in Tsarist Russia and the Soviet Union, 1789 – 1923* (Toronto: University of Toronto Press, 2002), 5.

[12] Rempel, *A Mennonite Family*, 263.

[13] Harry Loewen, *No Permanent City: Stories from Mennonite History and Life* (Waterloo, Ontario: Herald Press, 1993), 116.

[14] Ibid, 123.

[15] Frank H. Epp, *Mennonite Exodus*, 27.

[16] Arthur Kroeger, *Hard Passage: A Mennonite Family's Long Journey from Russia to Canada* (Edmonton, The University of Alberta Press), 13.

[17] Statistics are cited by Cornelius J. Dyck, *An Introduction to Mennonite History, 3rd ed.* (Waterloo, Ontario, Herald Press, 1993), 182. Statistics cited are attributed to Al Reimer, "Peasant Aristocracy: The Mennonite *Gutsbesitzertum* in Russia," *Journal of Mennonite Studies*, vol. 8, 1990.

[18] Dyck, *Mennonite History*, 182, 183.

[19] Ibid, 14.

[20] Ibid, 212.

[21] Edgar Rogalski, translator and editor, *Diary of Johann Neufeld and Barbara Funk Neufeld: From Russian Revolution to Pioneer Life in Peace River, Alberta* (2009), 1,2.

[22] Kroeger, *Hard Passage*, 76,77.

[23] Ibid, 78.

[24] Victor Peters & Jack Thiessen, *Mennonite Names* (Marburg: N. G. Elwert Verlag, 1987), 94.

[25] Thiessen, Richard D. "Klein Lichtenau (Pomeranian Voivodeship, Poland)." *Global Anabaptist Mennonite Encyclopedia Online*. December 2012.

[26] Helmut T. Huebert, *Molotschna Historical Atlas* (Winnipeg, Springfield Publishers, 2003), 159.

[27] Ibid, 173.